William Shakespeare

Twelfth Night

Edited by

John Russell Brown

APPLAUSE
NEW YORK • LONDON

The Applause Shakespeare Library
Twelfth Night

Edited with Commentary by John Russell Brown
General Series Editor: John Russell Brown
Copyright © 2001 Applause Books

Library of Congress Cataloging-in-Publication Data

Library of Congress Card Number: 00-111096

British Library Cataloging-in-Publication Data
A catalog record for this book is available from the British Library.

ISBN: 1-55783-389-3

APPLAUSE THEATRE BOOKS
151 W46th Street, 8th Floor
New York, NY 10036
Phone: (212) 575-9265
FAX: (646) 562-5852
email: info@applausepub.com

COMBINED BOOK SERVICES LTD.
Units I/K, Paddock Wood Distribution Centre
Paddock Wood, Tonbridge, Kent TN 12 6UU
Phone: (44) 01892 837171
Fax: (44) 01892 837272

SALES & DISTRIBUTION, HAL LEONARD CORP.
7777 West Bluemound Road, P.O. Box 13819
Milwaukee, WI 53213
Phone: (414) 774-3630
Fax: (414) 774-3259
email: halinfo@halleonard.com
internet: www.halleonard.com

Table of Contents

General Preface to the Applause Shakespeare Library

This edition is designed to help readers see and hear the plays in action. It gives an impression of how actors can bring life to the text and shows how certain speeches, movements, or silences take on huge importance once the words have left the page and become part of a performance. It is a theatrical edition, like no other available at this time.

Everyone knows that Shakespeare wrote for performance and not for solitary readers or students in classrooms. Yet the great problem of how to publish the plays so that readers can understand their theatrical life is only beginning to be tackled. Various solutions have been tried. The easiest— and it is an uneasy compromise—is to commission some director or leading actor to write a preface about the play in performance and print that at the beginning of the volume, followed by a critical and historical introduction, the text and notes about verbal difficulties, a textual introduction, and a collation of variant reading as in any other edition. Another easy answer is to supply extensive stage directions to sort out how characters enter or exit and describe any gestures or actions that the text explicitly requires. Both methods give the reader little or no help in realizing the play in performance, moment by moment, as the text is read.

A more thorough-going method is to include some notes about staging and acting among the annotations of meaning, topical references, classical allusions, textual problems, and so forth. The snag here is that the theatrical details make no consecutive sense and cannot deal with the larger issues of the build-up of conflict or atmosphere, the developing impression of character, or the effect of group and individual movement on stage. Such notes offer, at best, intermittent assistance.

In the more expensive one-volume editions, with larger-than-usual formats, yet another method is used to include a stage history of the play showing how other ages have staged the play and describing a few recent productions that have been more than usually successful with the critics. The snag here is that unavailable historical knowledge is required to interpret records of earlier performances. Moreover, the journalistic accounts of productions which are quoted in these histories are liable to emphasize what is unusual in a production rather than the opportunities offered to actors in any production of the play, the text's enduring theatrical vitality. In any case, all this material is kept separate from the rest of the book and not easily consulted during a reading of the text.

The Applause Shakespeare goes further than any of these. It does the usual tasks expected of a responsible, modern edition, but adds a very special feature: a continuous commentary on the text by a professional director or a leading actor that considers the stage life of the play as its action unfolds. It shows what is demanded from the actors—line by line where necessary—and points out what decisions about interpretation have to be made and the consequences of one choice over another. It indicates where emotional climaxes are placed—and where conflicting thoughts in the character's mind create subtextual pressures beneath the words. Visual statements are noted: the effect of groups of figures on stages, of an isolated figure, or of a pair of linked figures in a changing relationship; the effect of delayed or unexpected entries, sudden departures, slow or processional exuents, or a momentarily empty stage. Everything that happens on stage comes within the notice of this commentary. A reader can "feel" what the play would be like in action.

What the commentary does not do is equally important from the reader's point of view. It does not try to provide a single theatrical reading of the text. Rather if offers a range of possibilities, a number of suggestions as to what an actor might do. Performances cannot be confined to a single, unalterable realization: rather, each production is continually discovering new potential in a text, and it is this power of revelation and revaluation that the commentary of the Applause Shakespeare seeks to open up to individual readers. With this text in hand, the play can be produced in the theatre of the mind, creating a performance suitable to the moment and responsive to individual imaginations. As stimulus for such recreations, the commentary sometimes describes the choices that particular actors or directors made in famous productions, showing what effect words or physical performances have achieved. The purpose here is to supplement what a reader might supply from his or her own experience and imagination, and also to suggest ways in which further research might discover more about the text's theatrical life.

The commentary is printed in a wide column on the page facing the text itself, so that reference can be quickly made at any particular point or, alternatively, so that the commentary can be read as its own narrative of the pay in action. Also, to the right of the text are explanations of difficult words, puns, multiple meanings, topical allusions, references to other texts, etc. All of these things will be found in other editions, but here it is readily accessible without the eye having to seek out the foot of the page or notes bunched together at the rear of the volume. The text is modernized in spelling. Both stage directions and punctuation are kept to a minimum—enough to make reading easy, but not so elaborate that readers are prevented from giving life to the text in whatever way they choose. As an aid to reading aloud, speech-prefixes are printed in full and extra space used to set speeches apart from each other; when the text is read silently, each new voice can register clearly. At the rear of the book, an extended note explains the authority for the text and a collation gives details of variant readings and emendations.

In many ways the Applause Shakespeare is a pioneering edition, responding to an old challenge in a new way and trying to break down barriers to understanding that have proved very obstinate for a long time. Further volumes are in preparation and editorial procedures are being kept under review. Reports on the usefulness of the edition, and especially of its theatrical commentary, would be most welcome. Please write to John Russell Brown, c/o Applause Books, 151 West 46th Street, 8th Floor, New York, NY 10036.

INTRODUCTION

Twelfth Night is one of the simplest of Shakespeare's plays to enjoy, but possesses many moments which encourage a very penetrating attention or open up vistas of strange possibilities. Every playgoer, reader, and actor can have an adventure with this play.

The very title of the comedy advertises a double nature. In Shakespeare's day, Twelfth Night, or the feast of the Epiphany on January 6, was observed in England and throughout Europe as the last day of the Christmas festivities. A "King" or "Lord of Misrule" would be chosen by chance or by election, so that a servant might act for one day as master of the household and preside at a feast in the great hall. With drinking, toasts, games, mock trials, divination, dancing, and processions, it was a brief occasion for high spirits, feasting, and disguises. Winter was an especially dark and dead time of year when there was no electricity or oil-fired furnaces: people would gather round hearths and wrap up well to go out walking or riding. But at Twelfth Night, traditional ceremonies and rituals were concerned with rebirth and looking forward to harvest, seeking to avert diseases and ensure plentiful crops. In the play named after this festival, there is not much dancing and only one scene of corporate singing—and even that is interrupted as it grows toward its boisterous conclusion—but the Twelfth Night revelry is represented by various disguises and the reversal of roles between master and servant: Malvolio, the servant, dreams of being "Count Malvolio" and begins his performance; Olivia does she "knows not what" when she loves a servant rather than master; Orsino loves someone who serves him and whom, by the end of the play, he is ready to serve as his chosen "queen"; Antonio takes pleasure in dangerous service of Sebastian, a young man whom he has saved from the sea, and Sebastian lightheartedly becomes Antonio's "purse-bearer." Various reversals of luck, changes from sunlight to dark prison, and from the threat of death to life, and numerous mistakes of identity and intention are all appropriate to a festival comedy.

The Lord of Misrule is, perhaps, Feste, the fool whose very name is a form of "*Fête*" or "Feast." He seems to be a "merry fellow" who cares for nothing, but he sits in judgment on each of the other characters and through crazy and complicated jesting tells them the "truth" about their lives. He himself does "care for something," but what that is remains a secret, not to be revealed even in his last riddling, childlike, and cynical song with which he concludes the festival-play. While Feste remains to sing of the rain that "raineth every day," some, at least, of his subjects are determined to make a "solemn combination" of their "dear souls" when "golden time convents"— hopefully bringing all their stories together in the sunshine.

As soon as one tries to cast the play for performance, such paradoxes come into focus. Sir Toby is a knight, and proud of it, yet we are told that he marries a chambermaid for a joke. He is often drunk but swears that he "hates" a drunkard. Malvolio is a steward and yet he rehearses his behavior for more than half-an-hour before the day's work begins; not only does he think himself the most attractive man in the world, he also acts as if this were true. Olivia is a young heiress who has lost father, mother, and brother and who shuts herself up in her own house for seven years to avoid all men, and then she falls in love with someone else's servant as soon as they look at each other. Orsino is a duke who exercises great responsibility and has fought a sea battle, and then finds that he wants to murder a boy. Viola, who is disguised as this boy for most of the play, is sometimes like "patience on a monument, smiling at grief" and, at other times, "saucy" and "rude," or "fearful" and "mad;" in the last scene, she is both "jocund [and] apt" and willing to die. The demands placed on actors are as large as they are con- flictingly various. Henry Irving, who cast himself as Malvolio and Ellen Terry as Viola in his own production of the play, confessed afterwards that he ought never to have attempted it without having "three great comedians" in his company as well.[1]

When this comedy is staged in a theater with modern scenery and lights, the stage designer will also find two conflicting aspects to the task. The scene to be created is "Illyria," which is actually on the east coast of the Adriatic Sea, but more important than geographic and historical accuracy will be the need to give to the land that Orsino governs a double setting: a wild seacoast and the comfortable English countryside. There are allusions in the text to dangerous seas, "barren mountains," and political conflict and danger on the one hand and, on the other, to "sweet beds of flowers," squash, peascod, willow, beagle, roses, violets, yews, and a box tree. Characters talk about shipwreck, pirates, fights at sea and summary arrests, and also about

---

[1]   Ellen Terry, *The Story of My Life* (London: Hutchinson, 1908), p. 232.

daylight, open fields, harvest, ripeness, oxen and wain-ropes, and the songs of nightingales, daws, and owls. There is a prison as well as a house and garden. Devils, fiends, and hell occupy men's minds as do a "holy man," the "good life," and "devotion."

The last scene of the play is complicated in its stage business, with many comings and goings and careful postponements of the full comical conclusion. Disguises are dropped and misunderstandings resolved only when it is abundantly clear that the twelfth-night festival of folly has led each character to a manifestation of "What they will." Through madness, folly, confusion, revels, and disguises, the "truth," as Shakespeare calls it, has become progressively apparent. Sebastian provides a clue to this basic movement in the play when he promises Olivia that "having sworn truth" he "ever will be true." Orsino's last words make the same point (speaking to Viola as if to Cesario, his servant):

> But when in other habits you are seen,
> Orsino's mistress, and his fancy's queen. (v.i.370-1)

The servant is to be the mistress, and she will rule the master's "fancy," that strange, demanding, and "fantastic" source of what each character "wills."

The "will," alluded to in the play's subtitle—*Twelfth Night; or What You Will*—is that part of the human comedy in which discordant forces, images, and appearances find their single truth. When this play is performed, each member of the cast has to create an impression that his strangest words and actions are based on a strong, imaginative response to his fellow characters and the action of the play. For all the simple, domestic occurrences of the play, its conventional encounters between lovers, masters, and servants, and its madness and folly, each character is based on an individual, imaginative life—on "what they will," or wish, or desire, on what must happen if their inner "truth" is to be realized. (The word "will," for Shakespeare, encompassed all these meanings.) In one sense *Twelfth Night* is a comedy of unmasking: a winter celebration of new life which gives release to what is usually confined. Each character has moments of "folly," "madness," "frenzy," "anger," "uncivil rule," or "wonder," which are the outward "shapes" of fancy and the "will" as they struggle to be expressed, and by the end of the play the audience has been given opportunities to recognize the sustaining power of each individual, imaginative truth, the still center of each being.

Viola, disguised as Cesario, gives a warning to Olivia that may be taken as a motto for the whole play, and a warning to reader, actor, director, and critic:

> — I prithee tell me what thou think'st of me.
> — That you do think you are not what you are.
> — If I think so, I think the same of you.
> — Then think you right: I am not what I am.
> — I would you were as I would have you be.
> — Would it be better, madam, than I am?
>   I wish it might, for now I am your fool.   (III.i.132-138)

There are numerous episodes in the comedy that can be enjoyed with ease and immediate pleasure—evocations of beauty and assertions of desire, teasing and lovemaking, comic mistakes, practical jokes, absurd behavior, dramatic changes of fortune, displays of temperament, cunning, and enjoyment—but the comedy is also a riddle in that characters and statements are "not what they are." Shakespeare has created moments when the picture seems to go out of focus, and then the audience is invited to look more deeply and narrowly, and sometimes more widely, at what is happening.

In the theater, this play has had great and varied success. The commentary to this edition testifies to details of some famous performances and shows how single parts are capable of many interpretations. In earliest records, Malvolio dominated performances of the play, and yet, from late in the nineteenth century onwards, actresses such as Julia Marlowe, Ellen Terry, Peggy Ashcroft, Katharine Hepburn, and Dorothy Tutin have shown that Viola can usurp that position and this is often the case today. When Sir Toby and Sir Andrew are strongly cast and allowed to elaborate their performances, the romantic wooing as well as the gulling of the steward can take second and third places to well-practised clowning and highly detailed character-acting. In this century, Alec Guinness and Michael Redgrave as Sir Andrew, and Robert Livesey and Leon Ouartermaine as Sir Toby have given performances comparable with those praised by Charles Lamb at the beginning of the eighteenth century as the height of an English comic tradition. Feste, the outsider, the singer, and the fool, can also dominate the play, especially when a director such as Tyrone Guthrie or Terry Hands, has been determined to emphasize the melancholy strand running through the play.

In effect, it is the actors' play rather than the director's, for each character in turn is given sensitively written moments when he or she must control the whole theater by sheer acting. Most of the characters have been given silences, simple yet climactic words, physical actions, or delayed reactions all of which are left open to individual realization. So actors can put their own stamp on their parts and give performances grounded in their own personalities, their entire "presence" or actual being. Even the last scene, which brings almost all the characters onstage together, does not lead to a climactic group effect, like the dances and songs at the end of *Love's Labor's Lost*, *As You Like It*, or *Much Ado About Nothing*, or like the group jesting at the end of *The Merchant of Venice*. Rather this comedy ends with a sequence of precise, individual confrontations, as "will" meets "will" and makes clear its own "truth."

The time in which the action unfolds is said to be three months, but the various events portrayed could fit into two successive days, each shown at morning, noon, and afternoon, and the first day passing into midnight. Time passes lightly in this play, but with a consciousness of all the varying qualities of each day. So the considerable complications and resolutions of the plot should be accomplished with the ease and inevitability of the passing of time, and yet with an awareness of the variable resources of individual imaginations.

The earliest evidence for the existence of this play is the record of a performance in the Great Hall of the Middle Temple in London on February 2, 1602. This hall still survives, although damaged in an air raid during the Second World War. Against the ornately carved oak paneling of this dining and assembly room for lawyers and law students, Shakespeare's Illyrian comedy was brought to life as a special and private entertainment. Although it was new to John Manningham who recorded this performance, a few topical references and literary borrowings argue that it had been written a year or more earlier. Probably it had already been seen at the Globe Theatre and at court in the season of 1600-01. Certainly it was revived at court in 1618, and again in 1623 under the title of *Malvolio*.

For the source of the main romantic story, Shakespeare almost certainly read Barnabe Riche's story of Apolonius and Silla in his *Farewell to the Military Profession* (1581). He may have read further and earlier versions of the same tale and some of the plays using the same basic material. Shipwreck and the subsequent confusion of twins were common elements in romance and in Plautine comedy, and Shakespeare had used them before in *The Comedy of Errors*. The device of a girl disguised as a page serving the man she loves was also common, and in *The Two Gentlemen of Verona* Shakespeare had already explored some of its dramatic possibilities. The Italian comedy *Gl'Ingannati* (*The Deceived*), performed at Siena in 1531, has numerous features in common with *Twelfth Night*, and its Induction has a Fabio, a Malevolti, and a reference to "*Ia notte di Beffana*" or Epiphany.[2]

For the scenes involving Malvolio, no one source has been identified, and here Shakespeare probably relied on his own general reading, his memory of theatrical gulling episodes, and his own observation of life in the households of Elizabethan gentlemen.[3] Sir Toby Belch represents many younger sons of his own time, born into noble families but lacking an inheritance and so starting life as soldiers; when too old for their profession—and that might be in their early thirties—such men could only fall back on living with relatives and idling time away. So the young Olivia has to tolerate her uncle and his casual acquaintance, Sir Andrew, whom he introduces to her house. This younger knight has a small patrimony but little or no knowledge of how to make use of it; he is representative of scores of such young men who left their homes to make some kind of fortune only to be tricked out of their money by less congenial means than Sir Toby's confidence tricks. Malvolio is an ambitious man, relying on his own "good parts" and sense of duty; as such, he is invaluable to his mistress but isolated from the gentry and from the "lesser" servants. Several actual identifications have been suggested for the would-be upwardly mobile Malvolio; the most elaborately worked out is Sir William Knollys, a less lowly steward who was Comptroller of the Queen's household.[4] Maria, the gentlewoman who acts as Olivia's personal maid, and Fabian, the servant of some education who carries a grudge against Malvolio for interfering with a bearbaiting amusement, are also familiar figures of an English country-gentleman's establishment and help to account for the wide range of domestic and countryside references in this play.

Feste also has a place in the same social setting as a licensed fool. Here

---

2 G.Bullough, *Narrative and Dramatic Sources of Shakespeare* (London: Routledge & Kegan Paul, 1958), Vol. 2, pp. 269-85.

3 See J. W. Draper, *The Twelfth Night of Shakespeare's Audience* (Stanford, Cal.: Stanford University Press, 1950).

4 Leslie Hotson, *The First Night of "Twelfth Night"* (London: Rupert Hart-Davis; New York: Macmillan, 1954), pp. 93-118.

Shakespeare is more obviously indebted to theatrical tradition as well and to the expertise of clowns in the actors' company for which he wrote.[5] He must also have drawn on his own earlier writing for these actors, especially in *As You Like It* and the Launcelot scenes of *The Merchant of Venice* (in particular, III.v). Feste's dallying with words allows Shakespeare to relate the events of his main plots and the aspirations of each of his characters to a wide range of ordinary human activity of which he had direct experience: to piety, scholarship, lovemaking, war, avarice, hard work, old age and disappointment, and much more besides. By giving him songs and insisting that the fool has a "mellifluous voice," Shakespeare also introduced moments when immediate dramatic concerns are held back and the audience invited to attend to music and simple words, many of them taken from popular songs that anyone might know.

To most critics, *Twelfth Night* is the crown of Shakespeare's early work in comedy. Certainly it draws on many characters, themes, and situations that he had used before, from his first comedy onward,[6] and which reappear here in very different contexts and appearances. In *The Merry Wives of Windsor*, perhaps written in the same year, the setting is wholly domestic and favorite characters are, for the most part, older and more dispassionate. *All's Well that Ends Well*, *Measure for Measure*, and *Troilus and Cressida*, which followed within a few years, add a more judicial or "problem" frame to a romance story and explore more deeply the confrontation of death and deception; in the last named, the young lovers are brought to the field of battle and confront the breakdown of their love and trust. Thereafter followed the tragedies, *King Lear*, *Macbeth*, *Antony and Cleopatra*, *Coriolanus*, and *Timon of Athens*, and only in the last four or five years of his writing life, some nine or ten years after *Twelfth Night*, did Shakespeare return to comedy and its traditional characters of lovers, masters, servants, and fools; and then he placed them in very different contexts than that of this paradoxical, brilliant, riddling, and enjoyable masterpiece.

[5] See Leslie Hotson, *Shakespeare's Motley* (London: Rupert Hart-Davis, 1952), and, for a more general view of Feste's inheritance, W. Willeford, *The Fool and His Sceptre* (London: Edward Arnold, 1969).

[6] See John Russell Brown, *Shakespeare and His Comedies* (London: Methuen, 1957), pp.160-82.

Twelfth Night

CHARACTERS

ORSINO, Duke of Illyria

SEBASTIAN, brother of Viola

ANTONIO, a sea captain and
    Sebastian's friend

SEA CAPTAIN, Viola's friend

VALENTINE ⎫ attending on
CURIO   ⎭ the Duke

SIR TOBY BELCH, Olivia's uncle

SIR ANDREW AGUECHEEK

MALVOLIO, Olivia's steward

FABIAN   ⎫ attending on
FESTE, a clown ⎭ Olivia

OLIVIA, a countess

VIOLA, sister of Sebastian

MARIA, Olivia's waiting gentle-
    woman

LORDS, SAILORS, OFFICERS, MUSICIANS, ATTENDANTS, and a PRIEST

[SCENE   *Illyria.*]

ACT I

Scene i   *Enter* ORSINO, DUKE OF ILLYRIA, CURIO *and other* LORDS;
[MUSICIANS.]   [*Music plays and finishes.*]

DUKE   If music be the food of love, play on;
    Give me excess of it, that surfeiting°
    The appetite° may sicken, and so die.
                [*Music starts again, and is then stopped.*]
    That strain° again, it had a dying fall!°
    O, it came o'er my ear like the sweet sound   5
    That breathes upon a bank of violets,
    Stealing and giving odor.
              [*Music starts again, and is soon stopped.*]

Note:
Where there is reason to
  believe that Shakespeare
  used a word in a very special or rare way, the gloss is
  marked with an asterisk.

ACT I. Scene i

having more than enough
love, desire

melody/emotion   i.e., the
  music

1-16   The play begins with music instead of
words; but that music stops and then is started again,
and is stopped, started and stopped yet again. All
this is ordered by the duke, who reveals in doing so
his unsettled state of mind. By remaining silent, the
attendant lords and musicians accentuate the isolation of the lovesick man. Presumably, after line 8 the
musicians silently pack up their instruments and
depart; so they provide visual contrast to the duke on
whom dramatic development waits. Absorbed in his
own feelings, he talks to no one now, but addresses
the "spirit of love."

Enough, no more:
'Tis not so sweet now as it was before.
O spirit of love! How quick and fresh art thou,   10
That, notwithstanding thy capacity
Receiveth as the sea,° nought enters there,
Of what validity and pitch soe'er,
But falls into abatement and low price°
Even in a minute; so full of shapes is Fancy,°   15
That it, alone, is high fantastical.°

CURIO   Will you go hunt, my lord?

DUKE   What, Curio?

CURIO   The hart.°

DUKE   Why so I do, the noblest that I have.°
O when mine eyes did see Olivia first,   20
Methought she purged the air of pestilence°—
That instant was I turned into a hart,
And my desires like fell° and cruel hounds,
E'er since pursue me.°

Enter VALENTINE.

How now, what news from her?

VALENTINE   So please my lord, I might not be admitted;   25
But from her handmaid do return this answer:
"The element itself,° till seven years' heat,°
Shall not behold her face at ample view:
But like a cloistress° she will veilèd walk,
And water once a day her chamber round   30
With eye-offending brine:° all this to season°
A brother's dead love, which she would keep fresh
And lasting, in her sad remembrance."

DUKE   O she that hath a heart of that fine frame
To pay this debt of love but to a brother,   35
How will she love, when the rich golden shaft°
Hath killed the flock of all affections else°
That live in her?—when liver, brain, and heart,°
These sovereign thrones, are all supplied and filled—

This opening scene is often elaborately staged: for the Young Company at Stratford, Ontario, in 1988, "Orsino lay bare-chested on a table, massaged by one of his servants, while attending musicians played a melancholy air" (*Shakespeare Quarterly*, 40, 1989).

you take possesion (of everything) as the sea does

i.e., love makes all else seem trivial

sexual attraction

odd, changeable

Orsino's reference to "the sea" (12) is the first of several significant moments when its vastness, mystery, and danger are evoked in the play (see, for example, II.iv.97). The occurrence here suggests that the duke's sexual fantasies are potentially destructive.

17-24   Curio tries to change the duke's mood, but he responds with a savage pun and then the first mention of Olivia's name. Orsino speaks to himself again, fastening on the violence of hunting as an image for his sexual desire.

deer

(pun on *heart*)

cleansed the air of infection (like the goddess Diana)

fierce

(In classical story, Actaeon, the hunter, saw Diana bathing; she punished him by turning him into a hart)

At line 24, the duke turns quickly to Valentine, without giving him time to speak. Or perhaps Valentine hesitates before speaking, knowing he brings bad news and sensing his master's self-tormenting mood. Either way, the silent entry dramatically changes the mood and shows, visually and aurally, how unstable Orsino is.

sky   seven summers are
   past
nun

salty tears   preserve

27-33   Olivia's message has a gentler, more sustained rhythm than any other speech in this scene; its imagery is pious, rather then destructive or sensuous, and neatly elaborated. It is a quiet, yet strong, contrast.

Orsino must hold himself patient while Valentine is speaking; perhaps he has to struggle to do so at first.

34-42   The attendants will expect an angry response, but Orsino seems to be delighted. His complicated and fanciful description of his mistress expresses the excited mind of a romantic and intellectual idealist; and yet painful images remain.

Cupid's arrow

all other loves

(seats of sexual desire, intelligence, and feeling)

With line 40, Orsino's idealization of his intended relationship with Olivia is complete; either he sees himself as the object of her worship and con-

Her sweet perfections—with one self king?°   40
Away before me, to sweet beds of flowers:
Love-thoughts lie rich, when canopied with bowers. *Exeunt.*

Scene ii   *Enter* VIOLA, *a* CAPTAIN, *and* SAILORS.

VIOLA   What country, friends, is this?

CAPTAIN   This is Illyria, lady.

VIOLA   And what should I do in Illyra?
My brother, he is in Elysium°—
Perchance° he is not drowned. What think you, sailors?   5

CAPTAIN   It is "perchance"° that you yourself were saved.

VIOLA   O my poor brother, and so perchance may he be.

CAPTAIN   True madam; and to comfort you with chance,°
Assure yourself, after our ship did split,–
When you, and those poor number saved with you,   10
Hung on our driving° boat:—I saw your brother,
Most provident in peril, bind himself—
Courage and hope both teaching him the practice°—
To a strong mast that lived° upon the sea;
Where, like Arion° on the dolphin's back,   15
I saw him hold acquaintance° with the waves,
So long as I could see.

VIOLA   For saying so, there's gold.
Mine own escape unfoldeth to my hope°—
Whereto thy speech serves for authority°—   20
The like of him. Know'st thou this country?

CAPTAIN   Ay madam, well; for I was bred and born
Not three hours' travel from this very place.

VIOLA   Who governs here?

CAPTAIN   A noble duke, in nature as in name.   25

single object of adoration

trolling "king", or he pays homage to her regal will which he will have to respect. For the actor and director, choice between these two possibilities is an important factor in interpretation of the character and play.

Orsino sends his attendants away with a brisk order; fantasy, self-awareness, and indulgence now return quickly. He leaves the stage, alone, after the attendants.

Scene ii

1-3　　Instead of a fine lady in a cloister, which the audience expects after lines 20-40 of scene i, Shakespeare now presents a very young girl who has been shipwrecked and finds herself alone among unknown sailors in a strange land. This surprise is the first of many reversals of expectation in the play.

paradise
perhaps

by chance

The first three lines are simple but evocative. They are usually spoken after everyone has entered and the only sound is that of the nearby sea (perhaps half-expected after ll. 12-4 of scene i). The assonance and alliteration of the captain's first one-line speech, and the liquid sound of "Illyria," give a musical, unforced quality to his speech: so it holds attention and helps the dramatic situation to be realized quietly and suggestively.

what happened

drifting

way of coping
i.e., remained floating
(a poet rescued by a dolphin
　charmed by his song)
maintain his position

gives grounds for hoping

gives authoritative support

18　　Viola's immediate response to the captain's story is effectively simple in contrast to his elaborate and oddly graceful speech. The gift of gold from someone destitute and almost bereft of hope to someone unknown, together with Viola's hope for her brother, give an air of mystery and expectation to the scene—perhaps also of danger.

VIOLA What is his name?

CAPTAIN Orsino.

VIOLA Orsino: I have heard my father name him.
    He was a bachelor then.

CAPTAIN And so is now, or was so very late;°   30
    For but a month ago I went from hence,
    And then 'twas fresh in murmur°—as you know,
    What great ones do the less will prattle of—
    That he did seek the love of fair Olivia.

VIOLA What's she?   35

CAPTAIN A virtuous maid, the daughter of a count
    That died some twelvemonth since, then leaving her
    In the protection of his son, her brother,
    Who shortly also died; for whose dear love,
    They say, she hath abjured° the sight   40
    And company of men.

VIOLA O that I served that lady;
    And might not be delivered° to the world
    Till I had made mine own occasion mellow
    What my estate is.°

CAPTAIN   That were hard to compass,°   45
    Because she will admit no kind of suit,°
    No, not° the Duke's.

VIOLA There is a fair behavior in thee, captain;
    And though that° nature, with a beauteous wall,
    Doth oft close in° pollution, yet of thee   50
    I will believe thou hast a mind that suits
    With this thy fair and outward character.°
    I prithee—and I'll pay thee bounteously—
    Conceal me what I am, and be my aid
    For such disguise as haply shall become   55
    The form of my intent.° I'll serve this duke:
    Thou shall present me as an eunuch° to him.
    It may be worth thy pains,° for I can sing
    And speak to him in many sorts of music,
    That will allow° me very worth his service.   60

recently

newly rumored

28-29 The revelation that Viola has heard of Duke Orsino already will heighten dramatic interest and suggest that she may be saying less than she might. Her immediate recollection that Orsino "was a bachelor" may indicate that he was intended to be her husband before the shipwreck; many actresses play the scene this way. Certainly, at this point the audience recognizes the coincidence and possible conflicts of the plot: romance and fantasy are afloat.

sworn to abandon

presented

42 Another instinctive cry, as at lines 3-5, 7, and 28. Verbally it is uncomplicated, but in tone and force it can express a full sympathy with Olivia's losses and, therefore, Viola's own helpless grief.

arranged my affairs so that my condition is less harsh

bring about

personal request

not even

even though

conceal

demeanor

47-65 An incomplete verse-line suggests a pause before Viola speaks with decision, clear imagery, and alert intelligence. The captain has provided detailed exposition, but Viola dominates the action by this purposeful and unexpected conclusion: she will now serve Orsino and not Olivia (compare I. 42). That she changes her mind after learning that Olivia will not admit the duke's suit suggests an instinctive desire to be close to him. That she thinks of pretending to be a "eunuch" shows that she is well aware of the sexual implications of her plan and the need to control them—whatever the captain or the theatre audience may think of her ability to do this.

suit my plans

castrato singer

i.e., Orsino may reward him

prove

A strange, secret resource or an instinctive confidence may be implied in lines 59-60, which are placed climactically. In the scene's conclusion, as at the end of I.i, the focus is on one person's inner, and partly unknown, intentions—apt exposition for a play subtitled *What You Will*

What else may hap, to time I will commit;
Only shape thou thy silence to my wit.°

CAPTAIN   Be you his eunuch, and your mute° I'll be:
When my tongue blabs, then let mine eyes not see.

VIOLA   I thank thee. Lead me on.   *Exeunt.*   65

Scene iii   *Enter* SIR TOBY BELCH, *and* MARIA.

SIR TOBY   What a plague means my niece to take the death of her
brother thus? I am sure care's an enemy to life.

MARIA   By my troth Sir Toby, you must come in earlier o' nights:
your cousin,° my lady, takes great exceptions° to your ill°
hours.   5

SIR TOBY   Why let her except, before excepted.°

MARIA   Ay, but you must confine yourself within the modest
limits of order.°

SIR TOBY   Confine? I'll confine° myself no finer than I am: these   9
clothes are good enough to drink in,° and so be these boots too;
an° they be not, let them hang themselves in their own straps.

MARIA   That quaffing and drinking will undo° you: I heard my
lady talk of it yesterday; and of a foolish knight that you
brought in one night here, to be her wooer.

SIR TOBY   Who, Sir Andrew Aguecheek?   15

MARIA   Ay, he.

SIR TOBY   He's as tall° a man as any's in Illyria.

MARIA   What's that to the purpose?

SIR TOBY   Why he has three thousand ducats a year.

MARIA   Ay, but he'll have but a year in all these ducats: he's a   20
very° fool, and a prodigal.

make your silence fit my plan

silent spectator

Scene iii

niece   objection   bad

object, with exceptions previously noted (mock legal)

bounds of proper behavior

i.e., clothe (pun on *finer*)

for drinking in/to drink out of

if (common Elizabethan usage)

release (from confinement)
/ruin

handsome, valiant

1 This is the third short scene at the beginning of this play, this one with only two and then three people onstage. Another difference is that mood is more relaxed: Sir Toby is "sure" (2), whereas Orsino had been "full of shapes" and Viola in need of assurance. But when Maria, Olivia's chambermaid, assumes control over the knight (for Elizabethans a notable reversal of social status), the audience is presented with another *Twelfth Night* reversal and a further display of "what you will."

There is no obvious occasion or motivation for their meeting; sometimes Maria enters to wake a late-sleeping Sir Toby (see lines 35), or to help him dress (see lines 9-11). Sir Toby, at the Old Vic in 1958, entered first with tumultuous "gulps and shouts," and was a "belching" comic boor. But Granville-Barker, in his *Preface* (1912, p. vii), argued that Sir Toby is a "gentleman by birth" who has been a soldier and it is idleness that leads him to excess: "the boredom of Olivia's drawing room, where she sits solitary in her mourning, drives him to such jolly companions as he can find." He thought it wrong to base a performance on the knight's surname. In line with this opinion, Patrick Wymark, at Stratford-upon-Avon in 1958, made Sir Toby younger than usual; he was spry, with a sense of style, appreciative of a "beagle, true-bred," and expert at fencing. A melancholy Sir Toby is also possible, knowing from experience that "care's an enemy to life": "lethargy" and forgetfulness come with his drunkenness; yet he "hates a drunken rogue" and needs company.

total

Sɪʀ Tᴏʙʏ   Fie, that you'll say so! He plays o' the viol-de-gamboys ,°
and speaks three or four languages word for word without
book,° and hath all the good gifts of nature.

Mᴀʀɪᴀ   He hath indeed, almost natural:° for besides that he's a   25
fool, he's a great quarreller; and but that he hath the gift of a
coward, to allay the gust° he hath in quarrelling, 'tis thought
among the prudent, he would quickly have the gift of a
grave.

Sɪʀ Tᴏʙʏ   By this hand, they are scoundrels and substractors°   30
that say so of him. Who are they?

Mᴀʀɪᴀ   They that add° moreover, he's drunk nightly in your
company.

Sɪʀ Tᴏʙʏ   With drinking healths to my niece. I'll drink to her as
long as there is a passage in my throat, and drink in Illyria;   35
he's a coward and a coistrel° that will not drink to my niece,
till his brains turn o' the toe, like a parish top.° What wench!
Castilliano vulgo!° for here comes Sir Andrew Agueface.

Enter Sɪʀ Aɴᴅʀᴇᴡ Aɢᴜᴇᴄʜᴇᴇᴋ.

Sɪʀ Aɴᴅʀᴇᴡ   Sir Toby Belch! How now Sir Toby Belch!

Sɪʀ Tᴏʙʏ   Sweet Sir Andrew!   40

Sɪʀ Aɴᴅʀᴇᴡ   Bless you, fair shrew.°

Mᴀʀɪᴀ   And you too, sir.

Sɪʀ Tᴏʙʏ   Accost, Sir Andrew, accost.

Sɪʀ Aɴᴅʀᴇᴡ   What's that?°

Sɪʀ Tᴏʙʏ   My niece's chambermaid.°   45

Sɪʀ Aɴᴅʀᴇᴡ   Good Mistress Accost, I desire better acquaintance.

Mᴀʀɪᴀ   My name is Mary, sir.

Sɪʀ Aɴᴅʀᴇᴡ   Good Mistress Mary Accost—

Sɪʀ Tᴏʙʏ   You mistake knight: "accost" is front her, board° her,   50
woo her, assail her.

bass viol (stringed instrument)

from memory/incorrectly

in their natural (unimproved)
    state/like a born idiot

taste

(a perversion of *detractors*)

i.e., do not *sub(s)tract.*

knave (lit., groom for horses)

whipping top for public sport

be serious (Castilians were
    notoriously dignified)

mouse (an endearment/scold)

i.e., accost

lady's maid (Toby takes *that* as
    a reference to Maria)

(as in a sea fight)

22-29   Although Maria's direct challenge (see line 18) had got a direct answer, Sir Toby now draws her once more into jests and pleasurable fantasies.

34-38   At the climax of his description of Sir Andrew, Sir Toby reverts (as he often will in the play) to his "niece," and to an expansive view of good fellowship in which he is ready to challenge anyone. "By this hand" (30) may indicate that his hand is already on his sword.

"What wench!" (37) can be spoken in many ways: as an invitation to kiss or as a familiar admonishment. But this intimacy does not prevent Sir Toby from seeing Sir Andrew and he at once assumes a mock sobriety to greet him. There is a playful conspiracy, if not agreement, between Sir Toby and Maria; a welcome contrast to other relationships, so far in the play.

39-49   The description of his character and, perhaps, an expectant silence as he makes his entry give Sir Andrew a "star" introduction. The three greetings he gives to Maria will be varied to develop this comic first impression.

Sir Andrew can be pathetic, feckless, slow-witted, or neurotic. At Stratford in 1958, Richard Johnson played him as a "paranoid manic-depressive, strongly reminiscent at times of Lucky in *Waiting for Godot" (Observer,* 27 April). Eleven years later at the same theatre, Barrie Ingham gave him a melancholy Scots accent: he was "no mere daft gull. His hopeless affection for Olivia is emphasized by pathetic gifts of flowers; his need for friendship...is suggested by his pathetic but curiously dignified appeals in the eyes and his occasional snatching up of the nearest female hand to kiss" *(Shakespeare Survey 23,* 1970). In 1987, also at Stratford, David Bradley's Andrew was "Bemused, bedraggled, and bewildered, unremittingly conscientious in his efforts

SIR ANDREW   By my troth I would not undertake her° in this
company. Is that the meaning of "accost"?

MARIA   Fare you well gentlemen.

SIR TOBY   And thou let part so Sir Andrew, would thou mightst   55
never draw sword again.

SIR ANDREW   And you part so mistress, I would I might never
draw sword again. Fair lady, do you think you have fools in
hand?°

MARIA   Sir, I have not you by the hand.   60

SIR ANDREW   Marry° but you shall have, and here's my hand.

MARIA   Now sir, "Thought is free": I pray you bring your hand
to the buttery-bar,° and let it drink.

SIR ANDREW   Wherefore, sweetheart? What's your metaphor?

MARIA   It's dry° sir.   65

SIR ANDREW   Why I think so: I am not such an ass, but I can keep
my hand dry.° But what's your jest?

MARIA   A dry° jest sir.

SIR ANDREW   Are you full of them?

MARIA   Ay sir, I have them at my fingers' ends:° marry now I   70
let go your hand, I am barren.°   *Exit.*

SIR TOBY   O knight, thou lack'st a cup of canary.° When did I see
thee so put down?

SIR ANDREW   Never in your life I think, unless you see canary put
me down. Methinks sometimes I have no more wit than a   75
Christian, or an ordinary man has; but I am a great eater of
beef, and I believe that does harm to my wit.

SIR TOBY   No question.

SIR ANDREW   And I thought that, I'd forswear it. I'll ride home
tomorrow Sir Toby.   80

SIR TOBY   *Pourquoi,°* my dear knight?

SIR ANDREW   What is "Pourquoi"? Do, or not do? I would I had

take her on

to keep pace with his more sophisticated companions, he was touchingly uncomprehending in his failure to do so...[He] never laughed. The pursuit of pleasure is a serious business: and he was sadly exploited by Sir Toby" (*Shakespeare Survey*, 41, 1989).

53-61   Sir Andrew loses his sense of the immediate occasion to consider the meaning of "accost," and Maria assumes the meeting is over. When he is roused by Sir Toby (55-56), he automatically repeats the admonishment he has been given with comical inappropriateness. But then he effects a surprise by making a more courtly address, careful of his own dignity (58). Maria easily deflates presumption, but Sir Andrew presses bravely on (60-61).

to deal with/on a string

sure (originally an oath, by the Virgin Mary)

serving counter in a storeroom for liquors

62-63   Some Marias bring Sir Andrew's hand so that it touches her body—a provocation which she knows will be lost on him.

thirsty/indicates impotence

(proverbial saying: "Fools have wit to keep out of rain")
caustic

66-71   Sir Andrew is again thinking hard, maintaining contact as best he can; but then Maria leaves for no stated purpose. In performance, Maria either makes a silent point of leaving him to Sir Toby's sport, or exits on Sir Toby's silent instruction.

I have jests in readiness
without more jests

a light, sweet wine

74-99   After Maria's parting shot, Sir Andrew's spirits are low. But, spurred on by Sir Toby, he tells what he "thinks" and, by line 79, is ready to consider action by forswearing beef. The actor can show physically the rebirth of some faint spirit; verbally, it is expressed at last in the resolve to "ride home tomorrow," so standing up to his earlier mentor. This is exactly what Sir Toby does not want to hear; so now there is a clear conflict of purposes.

why (Fr.)

Sir Toby tries to change Sir Andrew's purpose by speaking of Olivia, saying she will not match with anyone with too much "wit," and by addressing him as "man" to man. Confidence is renewed, expressed in a resolve to stay accompanied by expansive fantasies about himself (97-99). This

bestowed that time in the tongues, that I have in fencing, dancing, and bearbaiting: O had I but followed the arts!

Sɪʀ Tᴏʙʏ   Then hadst thou had an excellent head of hair.°   85

Sɪʀ Aɴᴅʀᴇᴡ   Why, would that have mended my hair?

Sɪʀ Tᴏʙʏ   Past question, for thou seest it will not curl by nature. °

Sɪʀ Aɴᴅʀᴇᴡ   But it becomes me well enough, does't not?

Sɪʀ Tᴏʙʏ   Excellent; it hangs like flax on a distaff;° and I hope to see a housewife take thee between her legs, and spin it off.   90

Sɪʀ Aɴᴅʀᴇᴡ   Faith, I'll home tomorrow Sir Toby; your niece will not be seen, or if she be, it's four to one, she'll none of me: the count himself here hard by, woos her.

Sɪʀ Tᴏʙʏ   She'll none o' the count; she'll not match above her degree,° neither in estate,° years, nor wit: I have heard her   95
swear't. Tut, there's life in't,° man.

Sɪʀ Aɴᴅʀᴇᴡ   I'll stay a month longer. I am a fellow o' the strangest mind i' the world; I delight in masques and revels sometimes altogether.

Sɪʀ Tᴏʙʏ   Art thou good at these kickshawses° knight?   100

Sɪʀ Aɴᴅʀᴇᴡ   As any man in Illyria whatsoever he be, under the degree of my betters; and yet I will not compare with an old° man.

Sɪʀ Tᴏʙʏ   What is thy excellence in a galliard,° knight?

Sɪʀ Aɴᴅʀᴇᴡ   Faith, I can cut a caper.°   105

Sɪʀ Tᴏʙʏ   And I can cut the mutton° to't,

Sɪʀ Aɴᴅʀᴇᴡ   And I think I have the back-trick,° simply as strong as any man in Illyria.

Sɪʀ Tᴏʙʏ   Wherefore are these things hid? Wherefore have these gifts a curtain before 'em? Are they like to take° dust, like   110
Mistress Mall's picture?° Why dost thou not go to church in a galliard, and come home in a coranto?° My very walk should be a jig: I would not so much as make water but in a sink-a-pace.° What dost thou mean? Is it a world to hide virtues° in? I did think by the excellent constitution of thy   115

exemplifies Orsino's comments on the "fantastical" shapes of a lover's "fancy" (see I.i.15-16); Sir Andrew might ape Orsino in behavior and speech here, for both men are prey to unsatisfied "will" or desire.

i.e., while art would not improve your *tongues*, with curling irons (*tongs*) it could improve your hair

(as opposed to art)

cleft stick on which wool is wound for spinning (proverbially, an emblem of a woman's occupation)

rank   fortune
i.e., hope for you yet

trifles (Fr., *quelque chose*; pun on *kick*)

experienced (?) (or Andrew excepts Toby as older)

lively dance in triple time

frisky leap
meat/sheeplike fool (Toby puns on *caper* = seed used for seasoning)
backward dance step*

gather

(topical allusion or familiar name; curtains protected pictures)
running dance

lively dance (Fr. *cinque pace:* pun on *sink*)   talents

109-23   Entering into Sir Andrew's thoughts of revels, Sir Toby is led on to his most sustained speech in this first scene. Most actors mime the various dance steps and so build up to a climax visually and physically, as well as verbally.

By the time Sir Toby talks of "my very walk," he has transferred the fantasy from Sir Andrew to himself. At the height of his performance, which literally leaves Andrew standing, comes a challenge

leg, it was formed under the star of a galliard.°

SIR ANDREW   Ay, 'tis strong, and it does indifferent well in a
dun-colored stock.° Shall we set about some revels?

SIR TOBY   What shall we do else? Were we not born under
Taurus?°   120

SIR ANDREW   Taurus? That's sides and heart.

SIR TOBY   No sir, it is legs and thighs. Let me see thee caper. Ha,
higher! Ha, ha, excellent!   *Exeunt, [SIR ANDREW dancing.]*

Scene iv   *Enter* VALENTINE *and* VIOLA *[as* CESARIO,] *in man's attire.*

VALENTINE   If the Duke continue these favors towards you,
Cesario, you are like to be much advanced; he hath known
you but three days, and already you are no stranger.

VIOLA   You either fear his humor,° or my negligence, that° you
call in question the continuance of his love. Is he inconstant   5
sir, in his favors?

VALENTINE   No, believe me.

                    Enter DUKE, CURIO, *and* ATTENDANTS.

VIOLA   I thank you. Here comes the count.

DUKE   Who saw Cesario, ho?

VIOLA   On your attendance my lord, here.   10

DUKE   Stand you° a while aloof. Cesario,
Thou know'st no less but all:° I have unclasped
To thee the book even of my secret soul.
Therefore good youth, address thy gait° unto her;
Be not denied access, stand at her doors,   15
And tell them, there thy fixèd foot shall grow
Till thou have audience.

born under the influence of a
dancing star

donkey-colored stocking

the Bull (zodiac sign, usually
supposed to influence neck
and throat)

that echoes his earlier speeches, and perhaps relates to Olivia: "Is it a world to hide virtues in?" Then he remembers Sir Andrew and the matter in hand: from his fantasy of the world as a delightful, open-hearted dance, Sir Toby reverts to being puppet master to a fool.

When encouraged, Sir Andrew blossoms: he "thinks" boldly (see line 107), corroborates his own praise (117-8), dares (wrongly) to correct Sir Toby (121), and bends all his efforts to dancing "higher" so that he is speechless on departure.

Scene iv

1-7   Viola, in her disguise as a boy, is at first silent; some actresses show her practicing male bows before Valentine's entry. But as she responds to comment, aware of broader and more personal issues, her answers seem almost to silence Valentine. Hers is clearly a different awareness, and the audience is invited to share it or guess at it, as in secret, before Orsino's entry.

temperament   in that

i.e., all except Cesario

i.e., everything

direct your steps

11-27   In I.i, Orsino had separated himself from silent attendants; so his singling out of Viola is at once especially meaningful. His speeches to Cesario are ornate even though they deal with intimate matters; but there are opportunities for both of them to look openly at each other from the start on "Cesario," "all," or "soul."

Performances must be nicely judged; too much expression of Viola's interest in Orsino (or of Orsino's in Cesario) can overweight the lines. Viola's

VIOLA   Sure my noble lord,
   If she be so abandoned to her sorrow
   As it is spoke, she never will admit me.

DUKE   Be clamorous, and leap all civil bounds,°   20
   Rather than make unprofited° return—

VIOLA   Say I do speak with her, my lord, what then?

DUKE   O then, unfold the passion of my love,
   Surprise her with discourse of my dear faith;
   It shall become thee well to act my woes: 25
   She will attend it better in thy youth,
   Than in a nuncio's° of more grave aspect.

VIOLA   I think it not so, my lord.

DUKE   Dear lad, believe it;
   For they shall yet belie thy happy years,
   That say thou art a man. Diana's lip   30
   Is not more smooth, and rubious;° thy small pipe°
   Is as the maiden's organ, shrill and sound,°
   And all is semblative° a woman's part.
   I know thy constellation° is right apt
   For this affair. Some four or five attend him;   35
   All if you will, for I myself am best
   When least in company. Prosper well in this
   And thou shalt live as freely° as thy lord,
   To call his fortunes° thine.

VIOLA   I'll do my best
   To woo your lady. [*Aside.*] Yet a barful° strife!   40
   Whoe'er I woo, myself would be his wife.   *Exeunt.*

Scene v   *Enter* MARIA *and* CLOWN.

MARIA   Nay, either tell me where thou hast been, or I will not
   open my lips so wide as a bristle may enter in way of thy
   excuse. My lady will hang thee for thy absence.

break all the rules of good
   behavior
profitless

first reply is simple; her second pointed and reasonable but, when the Duke uses more violent imagery
(20), she interrupts almost pertly, perhaps with an
edge of helpless exasperation. At lines 25-27, Orsino
speaks of Cesario's physical qualities so that, by
now, a degree of intimacy is required.

messenger's

ruby red*   voice
high and clear
like
character influenced by stars
   at birth

34-40   Orsino has been describing (and, presumably, looking at) Cesario, but it is not clear how much
tenderness or amazement, or playfulness, is
involved; the actor must make an important choice
here. He concludes this close encounter by speaking
of his own knowledge of Cesario's temperament:
("constellation" suggests idealization), so this is a
moment must involve a measure of trust, to which
Viola has no reply. Orsino then moves rapidly on to
the business of the proposed mission. With a quick
and extravagant promise, he leaves the stage.

with rights of free birth

possessions, position in the
   world

full of impediments* (legal
   usage)

This time his attendants are not asked to
follow, so they must stand waiting for Viola. The audience will recognize in her terse aside that the story is
ready to unwind.

Scene v

1-22   Feste first enters the play (silently or, possibly, with laughter) refusing to explain himself:
despite his fund of words, a measure of withdrawal is
characteristic of him. In Shakespeare's day, he

CLOWN   Let her hang me. He that is well hanged in this world,
    needs to fear no colors.°   5

MARIA   Make that good.°

CLOWN   He shall see none to fear.

MARIA   A good lenten° answer. I can tell thee where that saying
    was born, of "I fear no colors."

CLOWN   Where, good Mistress Mary?   10

MARIA   In the wars;° and that may you be bold to say in your
    foolery.

CLOWN   Well, God give them wisdom that have it; and those
    that are fools, let them use their talents.°

MARIA   Yet you will be hanged, for being so long absent: or to   15
    be turned away°—is not that as good as a hanging to you?

CLOWN   Many a good hanging prevents a bad marriage:° and for
    turning away, let summer bear it out.°

MARIA   You are resolute then?

CLOWN   Not so, neither: but I am resolved° on two points.   20

MARIA   That if one break, the other will hold; or if both break
    your gaskins° fall.

CLOWN   Apt in good faith, very apt. Well go thy way! If Sir Toby
    would leave drinking, thou wert as witty a piece of Eve's
    flesh° as any in Illyria.   25

MARIA   Peace you rogue, no more o' that. Here comes my lady:
    make your excuse wisely, you were best.   [*Exit.*]

    Enter LADY OLIVIA *with* MALVOLIO, [*and other* ATTENDANTS.]

CLOWN   Wit, and't be thy will, put me into good fooling. Those
    wits that think they have thee, do very oft prove fools; and I
    that am sure I lack thee, may pass for a wise man. For what   30
    says Quinapalus?° "Better a witty fool, than a foolish wit."
    God bless thee, lady.

OLIVIA   Take the fool away.

foe (lit., military flags; puns on *collar* = noose, *choler* = anger; and *colors* = excuses) prove that true

mournful, *color*less

i.e., where it dies as soon as it is *born*

natural wit (pun on *talons*)

dismissed from service

(proverbial saying: "Hanging and wiving go by destiny") make it bearble

convinced

loose breeches (Maria puns on *resolvsd* = fixed; *points* = laces, suspenders, line 20)

would make as clever a wife

(an invented name)

would be dressed in a long petticoat, like a child or an idiot; it would be made of hard-wearing, variegated cloth in dull, greenish colors. He is, therefore, marked at once as an outsider in society—an outcast, refugee, misfit, or critic. No one in the play takes him to be the congenital idiot his dress might proclaim, but he evokes varied responses. He is enjoyed as a lighthearted and "mellifluous" entertainer, and sometimes his sexual innuendoes and grotesque mockery of decorum draw others to share his jokes and point of view. Sometimes he is feared as an outspoken critic, or condemned as a tedious and meddlesome nuisance; occasionally he is envied for his lack of restraint. Shakespeare has ensured that when other characters react to Feste, they proclaim their own natures, revealing insecurity or confidence in meeting the challenge of his intrusive folly.

The quickness of the verbal interchange with Maria (each character having questions and some short answers) is heightened by the expectation of Olivia's entrance: perhaps much should be spoken in an urgent or exaggerated stage-whisper. Several times either Feste or Maria seems ready to break off (see lines 5,8,15): certainly, in contrast with previous scenes, here are two people sparring, briskly and familiarly, about death, boldness, fear, wisdom, folly, marriage, and nakedness, in a way that makes everything seem easy, spirited, and playful, even if wholly unsettled.

23-26   Until this point, attention has been focused on Feste but now, characteristically, he speaks so close to Maria's hidden interests that his victim has no adequate reply: in performance, this is a "moment of truth." Maria is Olivia's waiting-maid, but she leaves as her mistress enters, so marking her independence and leaving Feste without support.

28-32   It is not clear why Olivia enters at this moment, although Maria seems to have expected her. Often she is shown at her devotions as described in I.i.29-33, with Malvolio in officious charge of an elaborate ceremony; or she is fretful and restless (not unlike Orsino in I.i).

Feste riddles about wit and folly either to reassure himself, or to excuse himself to Olivia, or to comment on the action of the play as a whole (and so

CLOWN   Do you not hear, fellows? Take away the lady.

OLIVIA   Go to,° y'are a dry° fool! I'll no more of you: besides   35
you grow dishonest.°

CLOWN   Two faults madonna,° that drink and good counsel will
amend. For give the dry° fool drink, then is the fool not dry.
Bid the dishonest man mend himself, if he mend, he is no
longer dishonest—if he cannot, let the botcher° mend him.   40
Anything that's mended, is but patched; virtue that trans-
gresses, is but patched with sin; and sin that amends, is but
patched with virtue.° If that this simple° syllogism° will serve,
so; if it will not, what remedy? As there is no true cuckold
but calamity, so beauty's a flower.° The lady bade take away   45
the fool, therefore I say again: Take her away.

OLIVIA   Sir, I bade them take away you.

CLOWN   Misprision° in the highest degree. Lady, *cucullus non facit
monachum*:° that's as much to say as, I wear not motley in my
brain .° Good madonna, give me leave to prove you a fool.   50

OLIVIA   Can you do it?

CLOWN   Dexteriously,° good madonna.

OLIVIA   Make your proof.

CLOWN   I must catechize you for it, madonna. Good my mouse°
of virtue,° answer me.   55

OLIVIA   Well sir, for want of other idleness,° I'll bide your proof.

CLOWN   Good madonna, why mourn'st thou?

OLIVIA   Good fool, for my brother's death.

CLOWN   I think his soul is in hell, madonna.

OLIVIA   I know his soul is in heaven, fool.   60

CLOWN   The more fool, madonna, to mourn for your brother's
soul, being in heaven.—Take away the fool, gentlemen.

OLIVIA   What think you of this fool Malvolio, doth he not mend?

MALVOLIO   Yes, and shall do, till the pangs of death shake him.   64
Infirmity that decays the wise, doth ever make the better fool.

enough   caustic

improper, lewd

my lady (It.; pun on *mad*, see
   line 121)   thirsty

mender of clothes/bungler

(Olivia's virtue is patched with
   sin, his sin with virtue; both
   are *patched* [motley] fools)

artless/foolish   deduction

as adultery always brings dis-
   aster, so (single) beauty
   must perish

act as presenter or chorus). "Those wits" (28) can be
spoken to allude to the silent Olivia who is now making her first entrance and is thus the natural visual
focus of the scene. If Malvolio, bearing his staff of
office, precedes Olivia, Feste can aim his comment
at the "wise" steward as well.

34   Feste must stop or avoid the servants who
step forward to "take him away," and so gain fuller
attention for his audacious application of "fool" to the
"lady." He cannot be sure that he is reprieved until
line 51 or 53 ("Can you do it?" or "Make your proof"),
at which point the "fellows" probably release him.

mistake/wrongful arrest

a cowl does not make a monk

I only look a fool (*motley* =
   fool's patched clothing)

smartly

(term of endearment)

(perhaps echoing patched
   virtue of lines 41-43)

foolishness

50-62   For the "catechism," Feste probably goes
to Olivia pretending to be a priest. Most Olivias (and
their attendants) cross themselves on thinking of the
dead brother. Her reply (58) may be indignant, quietly shocked, or possibly spoken through tears.
However, the language of both fool and lady is pat-
terned and formal, and Olivia might well answer par-
rot-like, until she is told she is a fool. The end of the
catechism brings laughter (and relief) for everyone,
except Malvolio.

64   Malvolio's first sentence can sound sour
and vindictive, and may well stop the general laughter. The initial "Yes" is characteristically decisive; it

CLOWN   God send you sir, a speedy infirmity, for the better increasing your folly. Sir Toby will be sworn that I am no fox;°
but he will not pass his word for twopence that you are no
fool.

OLIVIA   How say you to that Malvolio?   70

MALVOLIO   I marvel your ladyship takes delight in such a barren
rascal; I saw him put down the other day, with an ordinary
fool, that has no more brain than a stone.—Look you now,
he's out of his guard° already: unless you laugh and minister
occasion° to him, he is gagged.—I protest, I take these wise   75
men, that crow so at these set kind of fools, no better than
the fools' zanies.°

OLIVIA   O you are sick of self-love, Malvolio, and taste with a
distempered appetite. To be generous, guiltless, and of free
disposition, is to take those things for birdbolts° that you   80
deem cannon bullets. There is no slander in an allowed fool
though he do nothing but rail; nor no railing in a known discreet man, though he do nothing but reprove.°

CLOWN   Now Mercury indue thee with leasing,° for thou
speak'st well of fools.   85

Enter MARIA.

MARIA   Madam, there is at the gate a young gentleman, much
desires to speak with you.

OLIVIA   From the Count Orsino, is it?

MARIA   I know not, madam; 'tis a fair young man, and well
attended.   90

OLIVIA   Who of my people hold him in delay?

MARIA   Sir Toby madam, your kinsman.

OLIVIA   Fetch him off I pray you;
he speaks nothing but madman.° Fie on him! [*Exit* MARIA.] Go
you Malvolio: if it be a suit from the count, I am sick, or not
at home: what you will, to dismiss it. [*Exit* MALVOLIO.] Now   95
you see sir, how your fooling grows old,° and people dislike it.

i.e., crafty and dangerous (like you)

draws quick attention to this hitherto silent figure. Possibly Malvolio thinks he is being funny.

without a defense (of wit)

provide opportunity

73-74   Malvolio directs attention back to Feste. The fool can choose what "face" to show: genuine melancholy, private mockery, rivalry, and so forth.

foolish servants of fools

little blunt arrows

78-83   With a sudden reversal, typical of this play, Malvolio and not Feste becomes the center of attention. If Olivia pauses after her first sentence, or if Feste delays his response, Malvolio's silence will mark him as deaf to criticism: it is not in his character to be speechless with shame.

privileged fool and judicious man can say what they like against others

may the god of trickery give you the gift of deception (i.e., I hope no one will take you for a fool)

91-92   Maria may be testing Olivia's determination to maintain strict mourning and seclusion; or she may be genuinely impressed by Cesario's appearance and his way of coping with Sir Toby.

i.e., speaks as a madman

92-100   After quick and dismissive orders, Olivia turns to Feste in a more considerate tone. He replies with double-edged compliment and more fooling: he is now in service again, an "allowed" fool and easily intimate. For a moment, Olivia and Feste are close together, but his allusion to her marrying (when she

stale

CLOWN   Thou hast spoke for us, madonna, as if thy eldest son
should be a fool.°—

Enter SIR TOBY.

Whose skull Jove° cram with brains, for—here he comes—one
of thy kin has a most weak pia mater.°   100

OLIVIA   By mine honor, half drunk.—What is he at the gate,
cousin?

SIR TOBY   A gentleman.

OLIVIA   A gentleman? What gentleman?

SIR TOBY   'Tis a gentleman here. [*Belches.*] A plague o' these   105
pickle-herring!—How now, sot?°

CLOWN   Good Sir Toby.

OLIVIA   Cousin,° cousin, how have you come so early by this
lethargy?

SIR TOBY   Lechery? I defy lechery.—There's one at the gate.   110

OLIVIA   Ay marry, what is he?

SIR TOBY   Let him be the devil and he will, I care not. Give me
faith,° say I. Well, it's all one.   *Exit.*

OLIVIA   What's a drunken man like, fool?

CLOWN   Like a drowned man, a fool, and a madman: one   115
draught above heat,° makes him a fool; the second mads
him, and a third drowns him.

OLIVIA   Go thou and seek the crowner,° and let him sit o' my
coz;° for he's in the third degree of drink, he's drowned. Go
look after him.   120

CLOWN   He is but mad yet, madonna, and the fool shall look to
the madman.   [*Exit.*]

Enter MALVOLIO.

MALVOLIO   Madam, yond young fellow swears he will speak
with you. I told him you were sick; he takes on him to understand so much, and therefore comes to speak with you. I told

(alluding to proverb: "wise men have fools for children")

has vowed to live single) may cause her to turn away again.

censor's change for *God*(?)
head (for drink; Med. Lat.;
  pun on *mother*)

103-10   The humor is lessened if played too broadly. Probably Sir Toby is determined to appear sober and, therefore, says as little as possible. When he does speak, he is anxious to be correct, but can only repeat himself drunkenly until he belches—which he blames on the herring. This loss of dignity causes him to lose contact with Olivia and he turns instinctively and with some relief to the fool.

drunken fool

i.e., uncle (term used of any close relative)

  For once, Feste speaks without wit (see line 107) to bring Sir Toby to his senses but this does not work, for Olivia has to call him twice, before reproving him. Comically, Sir Toby is then lost in his own hazy misunderstanding (line 110); he tries to steady himself by returning to the message he had entered to deliver.

i.e., to *defy* the Devil (as he defies lechery)

111-22   Olivia resorts to a simpler question, but Sir Toby finally loses all contact with reality, calling for "faith" as if the Devil were actually at the gate. Believing all difficulty has been resolved he stumbles or glides off, leaving Olivia still unanswered.

more than enough to warm him

coroner

hold an inquest on my kinsman

  This nicely varied "drunk scene," which has prepared the audience for Viola's entry, concludes with a valorous, carefree exit that sums up Sir Toby's attitude to life ("it's all one") and is another demonstration of the play's concern for what each character wills.

  Recognizing folly in another, Olivia then consults easily with the fool.

him you were asleep; he seems to have a foreknowledge of   126
that too, and therefore comes to speak with you. What is to
be said to him lady? He's fortified against any denial.

OLIVIA   Tell him, he shall not speak with me.

MALVOLIO   H' as been told so: and he says he'll stand at your   130
door like a sheriff's post,° and be the supporter to a bench,
but he'll speak with you.

OLIVIA   What kind o' man is he?

MALVOLIO   Why, of mankind.°

OLIVIA   What manner of man?   135

MALVOLIO   Of very ill manner; he'll speak with you, will you,
or no.

OLIVIA   Of what personage, and years is he?

MALVOLIO   Not yet old enough for a man, nor young enough for
a boy: as a squash° is before 'tis a peascod, or a codling°   140
when 'tis almost an apple; 'tis with him in standing water,°
between boy and man. He is very well-favored, and he
speaks very shrewishly:° one would think his mother's milk
were scarce out of him.

OLIVIA   Let him approach. Call in my gentlewoman.   145

MALVOLIO   Gentlewoman, my lady calls.   *Exit.*

Enter MARIA.

OLIVIA   Give me my veil; come, throw it o'er my face;
We'll once more hear Orsino's embassy.

Enter VIOLA.

VIOLA   The honorable lady of the house, which is she?

OLIVIA   Speak to me, I shall answer for her: your will?   150

VIOLA   Most radiant, exquisite, and unmatchable beauty—I
pray you tell me if this be the lady of the house, for I never
saw her. I would be loath to cast away my speech; for

billboard set up in front of a
sheriff's house

130-32   Viola is strictly following Orsino's (absurd)
instructions of I.iv.15-17.

i.e., like other men

133-35   Olivia is forced to question the "discreet"
Malvolio as carefully as she has her drunken cousin.

unripe peascod (peapod)
    unripe apple
i.e., at turn of tide, flowing
    neither way
sharply

139-46   Malvolio seems so obsessed by his own
wit that he is oblivious of Olivia's feelings: his laugh-
ably fastidious description contains a string of scornful sexual innuendos on pod, cod, and stand, and he
concludes with a thoughtlessly discourteous allusion
to the shrewishness of all women.

149-50   In this scene Olivia has already inter-
viewed a fool, a drunk, and a self-loving "discreet"
man. Now she veils herself to interview Viola, a girl
pretending to be a boy. Viola's question (149) raises
a laugh because the answer should be obvious; or, if
all the ladies are veiled, it will be funny in itself as an
attempt at businesslike (male) briskness (at line 187
Olivia says that Viola "began rudely").

151-65   The contrast between the complimentary
address of line 151 and Viola's simpler request for
help that follows immediately heightens the audience's awareness of disguise and of thoughts under-

besides that it is excellently well penned, I have taken great
pains to con° it. Good beauties, let me sustain no scorn; I am
very comptible,° even to the least sinister° usage.   156

OLIVIA   Whence came you, sir?

VIOLA   I can say little more than I have studied, and that question's out of my part. Good gentle one, give me modest°
assurance if you be the lady of the house, that I may proceed
in my speech.   161

OLIVIA   Are you a comedian?°

VIOLA   No, my profound heart: and yet (by the very fangs of
malice, I swear) I am not that I play. Are you the lady of the
house?   165

OLIVIA   If I do not usurp° myself, I am.

VIOLA   Most certain, if you are she, you do usurp° yourself; for
what° is yours to bestow, is not yours to reserve. But this is
from my commission:° I will on with my speech in your
praise, and then show you the heart of my message.   170

OLIVIA   Come to what is important in't: I forgive you° the praise.

VIOLA   Alas, I took great pains to study it, and 'tis poetical.

OLIVIA   It is the more like to be feigned; I pray you keep it in. I
heard you were saucy at my gates, and allowed your approach
rather to wonder at you than to hear you. If you be not mad, 175
be gone; if you have reason, be brief:° 'tis not that time of
moon with me, to make one in so skipping a dialogue.°

MARIA   Will you hoist sail sir? Here lies your way.

VIOLA   No, good swabber, I am to hull° here a little longer.—
Some mollification for your giant,° sweet lady. Tell me your 180
mind, I am a messenger.

OLIVIA   Sure you have some hideous matter to deliver, when
the courtesy of it is so fearful.° Speak your office.°

VIOLA   It alone concerns your ear. I bring no overture of war,
no taxation of° homage: I hold the olive° in my hand; my   185
words are as full of peace, as matter.

memorize

responsive*   unfair

lying speech. The "sinister usage" (156) is either the ladies' silence or their giggles.

By line 162, Olivia may sense something unreal in what is happening: Viola's first words of reply can be deeply felt and her return to business a form of self-defense.

reasonable

actor (see *part*, line 159)

supplant

(pun: *usurp* = wrong)

i.e., your hand in marriage

beyond my instructions

167-70 This speech begins with the first undoubted flash of Viola's own feelings, her "spirit" that Olivia will speak of at line 261.

release you from repeating

i.e., it is madness to stay; if
   you must speak, cut it short

i.e., I am not in the mood for
   such banter

float without sail

i.e., the small Maria (ironic)

179-81 Viola's jocular reproof to Maria shows a rise of spirits; she is enjoying her male role and prepared to press Olivia. By line 187 the lady's curiosity (at least) has been aroused.

since the formalities inspire
   such fear   business

demand for   (symbol of
              peace)

OLIVIA   Yet you began rudely. What are you? What would you?

VIOLA   The rudeness that hath appeared in me, have I learned
from my entertainment.° What I am, and what I would, are
as secret as maidenhead: to your ears, divinity;° to any   190
other's, profanation.

OLIVIA   Give us the place alone; we will hear this divinity.
[*Exit* MARIA *and* ATTENDANTS.] Now sir, what is your text?

VIOLA   Most sweet lady,—

OLIVIA   A comfortable° doctrine, and much may be said of it.   195
Where lies your text?

VIOLA   In Orsino's bosom.

OLIVIA   In his bosom? In what chapter of his bosom?

VIOLA   To answer by the method,° in the first of his heart.

OLIVIA   O, I have read it: it is heresy. Have you no more to say? 200

VIOLA   Good madam, let me see your face.

OLIVIA   Have you any commission from your lord, to negotiate
with my face? You are now out of your text.° But we will
draw the curtain,° and show you the picture. [*Unveils.*] Look
you sir, such a one I was this present.° Is't not well done?   205

VIOLA   Excellently done, if God did all.

OLIVIA   'Tis in grain° sir; 'twill endure wind and weather.

VIOLA   'Tis beauty truly blent,° whose red and white
Nature's own sweet and cunning° hand laid on.
Lady, you are the cruel'st she alive,   210
If you will lead these graces to the grave,
And leave the world no copy.

OLIVIA   O sir, I will not be so hard-hearted. I will give out
divers schedules° of my beauty. It shall be inventoried, and
every particle and utensil° labeled to my will:° as, item, two   215
lips, indifferent° red; item, two gray eyes, with lids to them;
item, one neck, one chin, and so forth. Were you sent hither
to praise° me?

VIOLA   I see you what you are; you are too proud:

reception

i.e., a sacred message

190   Some Violas make "maidenhead" an unintentional female slip out of male vocabulary and so gain a laugh from their recovery; but it can be a calculated attempt at intimacy to gain more attention.

194   Alone with Olivia, Viola returns to her prepared speech.

comforting

195-201   Olivia seeks to mock Cesario out of his prepared words and she succeeds. Viola's request to see her face is either the instinctive curiosity of rivalry or a calculated appeal to vanity in order to become more intimate with someone who is successfully keeping her distance and the advantage of her superior status.

in the same style (of theological discourse)

strayed from the text (of your sermon)

paintings were protected by curtains

at this time

206-12   Viola's answer (206) can have large effect as a comic deflation, or it can be gently self-amused, or jealously self-defensive. At lines 208-12, Viola makes full amends in compliment (Shakespeare marking the change by a return to verse); most actresses signal a new awareness by a brief silence just before speaking these lines.

indelible

blended

skillful

statements

article i.e., added as a codicil

fairly

appraise/flatter

213-20   Olivia runs on (still in prose), in excitement or self-defense, avoiding the new challenge and probably avoiding Viola's eyes. If she moves and Viola remains still throughout this speech, the latter's next monosyllabic, fully stressed verse-line will make a sober contrast, whether spoken in bitterness or with instinctive admiration.

But if you were the devil, you are fair.   220
My lord and master loves you: O such love
Could be but recompensed,° though you were crowned
The nonpareil of beauty.°

OLIVIA   How does he love me?

VIOLA   With adorations, fertile° tears,
With groans that thunder love,° with sighs of fire.   225

OLIVIA   Your lord does know my mind; I cannot love him.
Yet I suppose him virtuous, know him noble,
Of great estate, of fresh and stainless youth;
In voices well divulged,° free, learned, and valiant,
And in dimension° and the shape of nature   230
A gracious person. But yet I cannot love him:
He might have took his answer long ago.

VIOLA   If I did love you in my master's flame,
With such a suff'ring, such a deadly life,°
In your denial I would find no sense,   235
I would not understand it.

OLIVIA   Why, what would you?

VIOLA   Make me a willow° cabin at your gate,
And call upon my soul° within the house;
Write loyal cantons° of contemnèd° love,
And sing them loud even in the dead of night: 240
Hallow your name to the reverberate° hills,
And make the babbling gossip of the air°
Cry out, "Olivia!" O you should not rest
Between the elements of air and earth,
But you should pity me.   245

OLIVIA   You might do much. What is your parentage?

VIOLA   Above my fortunes, yet my state° is well:
I am a gentleman.

OLIVIA   Get you to your lord:
I cannot love him; let him send no more,—
Unless, perchance, you come to me again,   250
To tell me how he takes it. Fare you well:
I thank you for your pains.—Spend this for me.

no more than repaid
unequaled beauty

abundant*
i.e., like Jove's

223 Olivia's simple-worded question can be offhand, impulsive, taunting; or it can be spoken with a new, direct curiosity about Cesario/Viola and her fervent speech rather than out of any interest in Orsino's intentions. However spoken, her next, dismissive one-line statement (line 226) is in sober contrast.

of good reputation
physique

living death

233-36 Triggered by Olivia's unconcerned dismissal of Orsino, Viola's own love for him can inform and give force to this reproof. In turn, this prompts Olivia's simple, and probably instinctive, "what would you?"—with emphasis on *you*.

(emblem of a forlorn lover)
i.e., Olivia
songs   rejected

reverberating
i.e., echo

237-45 Viola's reply to Olivia's challenge starts without hesitation as if such matters were already in her thoughts. Her speech grows in power, sustained with full verse-lines which are without mid-line breaks. Images start conventionally, but soon encompass the dead of night, hills, air, and sky. The name "Olivia" is in contrast to this progression and some actresses hesitate before speaking it; alternatively, they may 'hallo' it softly, as if about to say or inwardly saying, "Orsino." The "0" following suggests that there is a break in Viola's thoughts after this word and a considerable increase of feeling
    Line 245 is an incomplete verse-line suggesting a pause in which Olivia responds without words; the outcome of the whole scene pivots on this moment of recognition.

class

248-54 Both Viola and Olivia break the verse-lines into short phrases now; both are controlling their inner feelings and seek some escape. Viola later describes what happens here (see II.ii.16-18).

VIOLA   I am no fee'd post,° lady; keep your purse;
    My master, not myself, lacks recompense.
    Love make his heart of flint, that you shall love;   255
    And let your fervor, like my master's, be
    Placed in contempt. Farewell, fair cruelty.   *Exit.*

OLIVIA   "What is your parentage?"
    "Above my fortunes, yet my state is well.
    I am a gentleman."—I'll be sworn thou art;   260
    Thy tongue, thy face, thy limbs, actions, and spirit
    Do give thee fivefold blazon:°—Not too fast; soft, soft!
    Unless the master were the man.—How now?
    Even so quickly may one catch the plague?
    Methinks I feel this youth's perfections   265
    With an invisible and subtle stealth
    To creep in at mine eyes. Well, let it be—
    What ho, Malvolio!

Enter MALVOLIO.

MALVOLIO   Here madam, at your service.

OLIVIA   Run after that same peevish° messenger,
    The county's° man: he left this ring behind him,   270
    Would I or not. Tell him, I'll none of it.
    Desire him not to flatter with° his lord,
    Nor hold him up with hopes: I am not for him.
    If that the youth will come this way tomorrow,
    I'll give him reasons for't. Hie thee, Malvolio.   275

MALVOLIO   Madam, I will.   *Exit.*

OLIVIA   I do I know not what, and fear to find
    Mine eye too great a flatterer for my mind.°
    Fate, show thy force: ourselves we do not owe;°
    What is decreed, must be—and be this so!   [*Exit.*]   280

paid messenger

255-69 The word "fervor" (see line 258) is direct and strong, suggesting that Viola has turned to face Olivia before leaving the stage. She is angry at Olivia's easy unconcern and also, probably, at her own helplessness and "contemned" love.

Olivia's mask drops as soon as she is alone: at the end of the most sustained and varied scene in the play so far, a young girl, in deep mourning, is left alone onstage and is at first silent (258 is an incomplete line). She now feels helpless too: she starts to speak by repeating Viola's words, but then comments and interrupts herself, contrasting thoughts rapidly following one another. Variations of rhythm and meter, together with contrasts between "blazon" and "plague," "perfections" and "stealth," all suggest contrary thoughts and feelings crowding and clashing together.

i.e., Cesario's voice, features, and so on, all proclaim him a gentleman

268 Malvolio's entry is so prompt that it may look as if he had been hovering nearby, ready to be called and having just supervised the departure of Cesario.

276 Malvolio's precision is characteristic of him. Laurence Olivier, playing the role in 1955, lit up this short speech "with all the chiaroscuro of character—pomposity, self-importance, servility"*(New Statesman,* 15 April). The effect was enhanced by timing and stress: "Madam!...I will." Among other phrases Olivier treated in this way were: "Yes! and shall do..." (I.v.64), "My masters! Are you mad? Or what? Are you?" (II.iii.77), "Go off! I discard you." (III.iv.81), "Lady, you have." (V.i.314). Olivier's Malvolio was a "plain unlikeable man" (*Times*, 13 April): he was a vulgarian but he was reasonably annoyed; he both envied and despised his "betters."

In 1823, Charles Lamb described the Malvolio of Robert Bensley claiming that the character is "not essentially ludicrous. He becomes comic but by accident...We must not confound him with the eternal old, low steward of comedy...Bensley, accordingly, threw over the part an air of Spanish loftiness. He looked, spake, and moved like an old Castilian. He was starch, spruce, opinionated, but his superstructure of pride seemed bottomed upon a sense of worth" *(Elia: Essays*).

However, the text also justifies a Malvolio who is a "turkey cock," a common "geck and gull" who is told to "shake his ears," or a fantastic who asks what "an alphabetical position portends" and speaks repeatedly "out of his welkin" (see III.i.53).

perverse, capricious

count's

fawn upon, spare

I'm being carried away because Cesario looks attractive

own

277-80 Olivia had called Malvolio before express-

ACT II

Scene i   *Enter* ANTONIO *and* SEBASTIAN.

ANTONIO   Will you stay no longer? Nor will you not that I go with
   you?

SEBASTIAN   By your patience,° no. My stars shine darkly over me;
   the malignancy of my fate might perhaps distemper yours.°
   Therefore I shall crave of you your leave, that I may bear my   5
   evils alone. It were a bad recompense for your love, to lay
   any of them on you.

ANTONIO   Let me yet know of you, whither you are bound.

SEBASTIAN   No, sooth,° sir. My determinate° voyage is mere
   extravagancy.°—But I perceive in you so excellent a touch of   10
   modesty, that you will not extort from me what I am willing
   to keep in; therefore it charges me in manners, the rather to
   express myself.°—You must know of me then, Antonio, my
   name is Sebastian, which I called Roderigo: my father was
   that Sebastian of Messaline, whom I know you have heard   15
   of. He left behind him myself and a sister, both born in an
   hour. If the heavens had been pleased, would we had so
   ended! But you sir, altered that; for some hour before you
   took me from the breach° of the sea, was my sister drowned.

ANTONIO   Alas the day!   20

SEBASTIAN   A lady sir, though it was said she much resembled me,
   was yet of many accounted beautiful. But though I could
   not with such estimable° wonder overfar believe that, yet
   thus far I will boldly publish° her: she bore a mind that envy
   could not but call fair. [*Weeps.*] She is drowned already, sir,   25
   with salt water, though I seem to drown her remembrance
   again with more.

ing her purpose in soliloquy but her plan seems fully formed as she gives brisk orders. Now, while she speaks of "fear", some Olivias weep for happiness, cry out, dance, or laugh. The short phrases completing the second rhyme suggest she should run of off-stage as if transported.

ACT II. Scene i

permission
my bad luck may spread to
you like a disease

truly   intended / limited
wandering about*

good manners require me to
give an account of myself

1-7   Cesario has just left Olivia, so that when Viola's twin brother enters, dressed as she was (see III.iv.342-6), the audience may well think that it is Cesario who now reenters opportuned by some unknown sea captain. In Elizabethan performances when very young men or boys played both Viola and Sebastian, identities might remain obscure longer. The juxtaposition of exit and entry reminds the audience, without verbal statement, of the complexity and fantasy of the plot.

The opening of the scene also echoes Viola's arrival in Illyria, but Sebastian has no hope that his twin "is not drowned" (see I.ii). His mood is darker and more restless: he is going somewhere, and yet nowhere; he recognizes Antonio's "love" (which is more than Viola finds in her sea captain), but tries to cut himself off from his company. However the complication and refinement of his prose speeches lend an air of unreality to this brief scene.

assault, breaking waves

highly valued
report

9-37   Sebastian has considerable exposition to effect but, once the scene is under way, syntax and word order give short, alert phrasing to much of what he says: the actor can give an impression of tension and instability. Sebastian's feeling for his sister is expressed by tears (the first that are actually required by the text) and these can provide an inarticulate center for the scene. He fights back to words wittily, as if trying to laugh at his own helplessness (see lines 25-27, 32-36).

The beginning of his last speech shows that the scene should be played as if Sebastian thinks his only hope for sanity or life is to be on his own: while Viola had sought engagement, Sebastian struggles to avoid it.

ANTONIO   Pardon me sir, your bad entertainment.°

SEBASTIAN   O good Antonio, forgive me your trouble.°

ANTONIO   If you will not murder me for° my love, let me be your   30
servant.

SEBASTIAN   If you will not undo what you have done, that is, kill
him whom you have recovered, desire it not. Fare ye well at
once: my bosom is full of kindness, and I am yet so near the
manners of my mother that, upon the least occasion more,   35
mine eyes will tell tales of me.° I am bound to the Count
Orsino's court. Farewell.   *Exit.*

ANTONIO   The gentleness of all the gods go with thee.
I have many enemies in Orsino's court,
Else would I very shortly see thee there.   40
But come what may, I do adore thee so,
That danger shall seem sport, and I will go.   *Exit.*

Scene ii   *Enter* VIOLA *and* MALVOLIO, *at several*° *doors.*

MALVOLIO   Were not you ev'n now with the Countess Olivia?

VIOLA   Even now sir; on a moderate pace, I have since arrived
but hither.

MALVOLIO   She returns this ring to you, sir. You might have
saved me my pains, to have taken it away yourself. She adds   5
moreover, that you should put your lord into a desperate
assurance° she will none of him. And one thing more, that
you be never so hardy to come again in his affairs, unless it
be to report your lord's taking of this. Receive it so.

VIOLA   She took the ring of me:—I'll none of it.   10

MALVOLIO   Come sir, you peevishly° threw it to her: and her will
is, it should be so returned. If it be worth stooping for, there it
lies, in your eye;° if not, be it his that finds it.   *Exit.*

VIOLA   I left no ring with her. What means this lady?

treatment (at my hands)

the trouble I have given you

cause my death in return for

betray me by weeping (like a
  woman)

38-42　Antonio has said little but was persistent
and sensitive so that Sebastian feels able to confide
in him. Now his soliloquy shows contrary impulses, at
first a decision to retreat and then, with a reversal
typical of this play, a decision to pursue. After line 40,
a brief silence can show Antonio accepting "what he
wills"; when he next speaks his resolve is complete.

　　Antonio's "I do adore thee so" associates
his feelings for Sebastian with Orsino's frustrated
love for Olivia (see I.v.224).

different

Scene ii

1-3　In some productions, Viola enters so
promptly that Antonio is in danger of following the
wrong boy—a development of the stage trick introduced at the beginning of II.i.

hopeless certainty

9-13　Malvolio probably withholds the ring until
"Receive it so"; by this time Viola is ready with a cool,
teasing falsehood. (But some editors emend line 10:
"She took no ring...")

　　The business of leaving the ring on the
floor is unusual: it can be comic, petty, outraged,
mock-dignified. At one time it was a tradition for
Malvolio to put the ring over the tip of a long wand of
office and let it slip down to the floor, so avoiding the
need of having to stoop to put it there.

impudently

view

14-38　Viola's questions and exclamations may

Fortune forbid my outside have not charmed° her.   15
She made good view of me; indeed so much,
That sure methought her eyes had lost her tongue,°
For she did speak in starts distractedly.
She loves me sure; the cunning of her passion
Invites me in this churlish messenger.   20
None of my lord's ring? Why he sent her none.
I am the man.° If it be so, as 'tis,
Poor lady! She were better love a dream.
Disguise, I see thou art a wickedness,
Wherein the pregnant enemy° does much.   25
How easy is it, for the proper false°
In women's waxen hearts to set their forms!°
Alas, our frailty is the cause, not we,
For such as we are made of, such we be.
How will this fadge?° My master loves her dearly;   30
And I (poor monster°) fond° as much on him;
And she (mistaken) seems to dote on me.
What will become of this? As I am man,
My state is desperate for my master's love.
As I am woman (now alas the day!),   35
What thriftless° sighs shall poor Olivia breathe!
O Time, thou must untangle this, not I;
It is too hard a knot for me t' untie.   [*Exit.*]

Scene iii   *Enter* Sir Toby *and* Sir Andrew.

Sir Toby   Approach Sir Andrew. Not to be abed after midnight is
to be up betimes; and "*Deliculo surgere,*"° thou know'st.

Sir Andrew   Nay, by my troth, I know not: but I know, to be up
late, is to be up late.

Sir Toby   A false conclusion; I hate it as an unfilled can.° To be   5
up after midnight, and to go to bed then, is early; so that to go
to bed after midnight, is to go to bed betimes. Does not our
lives consist of the four elements?°

put a spell on

she had been tongue-tied by
what she saw

be directed at the audience; if so, her relationship to the audience will be closer and more apparently open than that of any other character so far in the play. The frequent short phrases, parenthetical comments (31-35), and the general reflection of lines 24-29, indicate alert thought and feeling. Viola's self-criticism is half-mocking, half-encouraging; she realizes the dangers and absurdities of living by "what you will," as she commits herself to just that.

i.e., whom she loves

"The *look* with which [Ellen Tree] said 'I am the man' was perfect; but that little saucy tip of her head, with the playful swagger which followed it, though they 'brought down the house,' appeared to us to betray a forgetfulness of [the character of] Viola" (G. H. Lewes, 1850, quoted in A. C. Sprague, *Shakespeare and the Actors*,1944). Dorothy Tutin, at Stratford-upon-Avon in 1958, held back the laughter until "Poor lady!" (23).

resourceful Satan

good looking deceivers (i.e.,
men)

impressions (as of a seal)

work out

monstrosity (i.e., part man,
part woman)   love fool-
ishly

The role of Viola is open to both sensitive-romantic and comic-absurd interpretations, the latter accentuated by gauche attempts to disguise her sex. The balance between the two varies with each performer: Julia Marlowe was "a Viola, all woman. She makes no attempt to play the boy. It may rob the mere intrigue of the play of verisimilitude, but how greatly it adds to its allurement…She is feminine in every phase of her." But she was also funny: "there is humor in the uplifting of her eyes, in her pose, in her voice. It is a subtle humor—there is no pointing of lines" *(Standard* , 27 April 1907).

profitless

Scene iii

(part of Latin tag from school-
book: "it is most healthful
to rise early")

1-2   Sir Andrew (conscious of the lateness of the hour) probably stumbles on after Sir Toby, so providing a basic contrast of performances. At first he is silent and submits to indoctrination, like a child at school.

tankard

(It was thought that men were
composed of varying pro-
portions of air, fire, earth,
and water)

5   The "unfilled can" can be the start of numerous pieces of comic business—Sir Toby is drunk and yet always lacks a drink: when he calls for "wine" (12), Feste enters, not Maria; when she does come, she brings reproof for "caterwauling" (64); when he again calls for drink (see line 107, she

SIR ANDREW   Faith, so they say;. but I think it rather consists of
eating and drinking.   10

SIR TOBY   Th' art a scholar! Let us therefore eat and drink. Marian,
I say, a stoup° of wine!

Enter CLOWN.

SIR ANDREW   Here comes the fool, i' faith.

CLOWN   How now, my hearts! Did you never see the picture of
We Three?°   15

SIR TOBY   Welcome, ass. Now let's have a catch.°

SIR ANDREW   By my troth, the fool has an excellent breast.° I had
rather than forty shillings I had such a leg, and so sweet a
breath to sing, as the fool has. In sooth, thou wast in very
gracious° fooling last night, when thou spok'st of Pigrogro-   20
mitus, of the Vapians passing the equinoctial of Queubus.°
'Twas very good, i' faith. I sent thee sixpence for thy leman.°
Hadst it?

CLOWN   I did impeticos thy gratillity: for Malvolio's nose is no
whipstock. My lady has a white hand, and the Myrmidons   25
are no bottle-ale houses.°

SIR ANDREW   Excellent. Why this is the best fooling, when all is
done. Now a song !

SIR TOBY   Come on, there is sixpence for you. Let's have a song.

SIR ANDREW   There's a testril° of me too. If one knight give a—   30

CLOWN   Would you have a love song, or a song of good life?°

SIR TOBY   A love song, a love song.

SIR ANDREW   Ay, ay! I care not for good life.

CLOWN   [*Sings.*] O mistress mine, where are you roaming?
                    O stay and hear, your true-love's coming,   35
                        That can sing both high and low.
                    Trip no further, pretty sweeting;
                    Journeys end in lovers meeting,
                        Every wise man's son° doth know.

answers with a plot against Malvolio (see line 119). Now Sir Toby seems ready for bed, but changes his mond to go offstage still seeking a drink (see line 167). So played, Sir Toby will be restless and dissatisfied and this mood will sharpen the many verbal references to desire and yearning.

measure of two quarts

But the scene is often played with liberal provision of drink; then the humor is more boisterous, and Toby more bullying and coarse.

9-10 As in his previous speech, Sir Andrew, with great and usually very intense seriousness, manages to counter Sir Toby with the most obvious truisms. However some actors play both lines as if he is already half-drunk and eager to keep up with Sir Toby.

i.e., picture of two asses Labeled *We Three*; the viewer makes the third

round (for three or more voices)

pair of lungs, voice

17-30 After another of his petty oaths, Sir Andrew blossoms in the fool's company, giving his longest speech in the play so far. He is then outclassed by Feste (with sour, aggressive wit), but this only increases his pleasure, so that he feels equal to Sir Toby (see line 30).

acceptable, winning

(invented names)

sweetheart

33 Sir Andrew may here echo the Bishops' Bible (1568), *Matthew* vi.25-34: "be not careful for your life, what ye shall eat, or drink..." (see also lines 9-10). So, unwittingly, he speaks wisdom like a wise fool, at the climax of a run of repartee.

I put the tip in my long fool's coat: Malvolio may smell out our fun, but cannot whip us. Olivia is a virgin, and we followers have little to drink (?)

34-47 The song is justly famous and written with great sophistication: simple monosyllables and fluent verse; contrasts between feminine and masculine line-endings; proverbial formality and light intimacy; an easy and yet tactful flirtation between amatory and moral meanings; opportunities for singing "both high and low;" a neat and strongly placed allusion to fools with "Every wise man's son;" and a thought-provoking repetition of the word *present* at the crux of the song. Dramatically, Shakespeare delayed the conclusive "Then come kiss me" until after "unsure" (a second negative statement) has sounded but still waits for its rhyme. In performance, the song is like an inset perspective within a larger picture: it shows great depth in little compass; and it holds back attention from more immediate concerns. The image of life presented here is both more vast and more securely contained than that in the play's lively dramatic action and dialogue.

sixpence (old, odd word)

morality (Andrew interprets this to mean the good things of life, line 33)

i.e., every fool (proverbial)

SIR ANDREW   Excellent good, i' faith.   40

SIR TOBY   Good, good.

CLOWN   [*Sings.*] What is love? 'Tis not hereafter;
   Present mirth hath present laughter;
   What's to come is still° unsure:
   In delay there lies no plenty;   45
   Then come kiss me, sweet and twenty,°
   Youth's a stuff will not endure.

SIR ANDREW   A mellifluous voice, as I am true knight.

SIR TOBY   A contagious breath.°

SIR ANDREW   Very sweet, and contagious, i' faith.   50

SIR TOBY   To hear by the nose, it is dulcet in contagion.° But
shall we make the welkin° dance indeed? Shall we rouse the
night owl in a catch, that will draw three souls out of one
weaver?° Shall we do that?

SIR ANDREW   And you love me, let's do't. I am dog° at a catch.   55

CLOWN   By'r Lady sir, and some dogs will catch well.

SIR ANDREW   Most certain. Let our catch be "Thou knave."

CLOWN   "Hold thy peace, thou knave" knight? I shall be constrained in't to call thee knave, knight.

SIR ANDREW   'Tis not the first time I have constrained one to call   60
me knave. Begin fool: it begins, "Hold thy peace."

CLOWN   I shall never begin if I hold my peace.

SIR ANDREW   Good i' faith! Come begin.   *Catch sung.*

Enter MARIA.

MARIA   What a caterwauling do you keep here? If my lady have
not called up her steward Malvolio, and bid him turn you   65
out of doors, never trust me.

SIR TOBY   My lady's a Cataian,° we are politicians,° Malvolio's a
Peg-a-Ramsey,° and [*Sings.*] "Three merry men be we." Am
not I consanguineous?° Am I not of her blood? Tillyvally,°

40-41   The two knights are now in agreement, so helping to hold the stillness invoked by Feste's song and including themselves in its mood. After the fooling, drunken stumbling, and Feste's surprise entry, this is a moment of indulgent harmony and reflection.

always

very sweet one

catchy song

if we hear by nose, the *breath* is sweet, not foul

sky

(proverbially, timid and psalm singing)

clever

51-55   Sir Toby is now exuberantly in the lead. In contrast, Feste is silent after his song: this is one of many opportunities for Feste to hold back and observe. Sir Andrew is jubilant and careless, forgetting his customary oaths.

57-63   The catch goes:
  Hold they peace, thou knave,
  And I prithee hold thy peace.
Much comic business is usually introduced: for example, Sir Andrew may start too late, sing too high or too low, go on singing long after the others (until they rejoin him to end in perfect unison, *fortissimo*), etc.

64-65   To gain attention, Maria may have to shout; or she may take hold of Sir Toby, for only he answers, in a mixture of further singing and boasting. With "Am I not consanguineous...not of her blood?", he strikes a more serious note, for he depends upon Olivia's hospitality and forbearance (see Malvolio's view of this, lines 83-88).

is from Cathay/is incredible tricksters

an old woman

related by blood   nonsense! (an old phrase)

67-70   The text quotes the first lines of two popular songs: one is found in George Peele's *Old Wives Tale* (1595); the other is *The Ballad of Constant Susanna*, which tells the story of Susanna and the

lady! [*Sings.*] "There dwelt a man in Babylon, lady, lady."   70

CLOWN   Beshrew° me, the knight's in admirable fooling.

SIR ANDREW   Ay, he does well enough if he be disposed, and so do I
  too. He does it with a better grace, but I do it more natural.°

SIR TOBY   [*Sings.*] "O the twelfth day of December."

MARIA   For the love o' God, peace!   75

Enter MALVOLIO.

MALVOLIO   My masters, are you mad? Or what are you? Have
  you no wit,° manners, nor honesty,° but to gabble like tinkers
  at this time of night? Do ye make an alehouse of my lady's
  house, that ye squeak out your coziers'° catches without any
  mitigation or remorse° of voice? Is there no respect of place,   80
  persons, nor time in you?

SIR TOBY   We did keep time sir, in our catches. Sneck up.°

MALVOLIO   Sir Toby, I must be round° with you. My lady bade me
  tell you, that though she harbors you as her kinsman, she's
  nothing allied to your disorders. If you can separate yourself   85
  and your misdemeanors, you are welcome to the house. If
  not, and it would please you to take leave of her, she is very
  willing to bid you farewell.

SIR TOBY   [*Sings.*] "Farewell dear heart, since I must needs be
  gone."   90

MARIA   Nay, good Sir Toby.

CLOWN   [*Sings.*] "His eyes do show his days are almost done."

MALVOLIO   Is't even so?

SIR TOBY   [*Sings.*] "But I will never die."

CLOWN   [*Sings.*] Sir Toby, there you lie.   95

MALVOLIO   This is much credit to you.

SIR TOBY   [*Sings.*] "Shall I bid him go?"

CLOWN   [*Sings.*] "What and if you do?"

devil take

naturally / like a born fool

Elders from the *Apocryhpha*, and is usually sung to a variant form of "Greensleeves." In performance several lines are usually used:

i. Three merry men, and three merry men,
And three merry men be we:
I in the wood and thou on the ground,
And Jack sleeps in the tree.

ii. There dwelt a man in Babylon
Of reputation great by fame;
He took to wife a fair woman,
Susanna she was called by name.
A woman fair and virtuous:
Lady, lady!
Why should we not of her learn thus
To live godly?

judgment   decency

cobblers'

suspension

go hang

blunt

76-78   Further words for "the twelfth day" are not known. All three characters usually join in repeating these words variously to provide a climax of foolery, lasting through Maria's remonstrance and Malvolio's entrance.

The steward is usually in a nightshirt, but also wearing his chain of office; he often carries a candle.

76-82   Silence greets Malvolio's string of questions: in the middle of twelfth-night revelry (see line 74), he has complained of license and claimed sanity (see line 76: "are you mad?"). Sir Andrew does not speak again until Malvolio has gone but Sir Toby is irrepressible, claiming a proper order in their singing. He probably turns his back on the intruder as he dismisses him contemptuously (line 82).

89-100   Knight and clown share and vary the words of another popular song, as in a vaudeville act: "Farewell dear love, since thou wilt needs be gone, / Mine eyes do show my life is almost done./ Nay, I will never die / So long as I can spy…"

SIR TOBY [*Sings.*] "Shall I bid him go, and spare not?"

CLOWN [*Sings.*] "O no, no, no, no, you dare not!"   100

SIR TOBY Out o' tune sir: ye lie.—Art any more than a steward?
Dost thou think because thou art virtuous, there shall be no
more cakes and ale?

CLOWN Yes by Saint Anne,° and ginger° shall be hot i' th'
mouth too.   105

SIR TOBY Th' art i' th' right.—Go sir, rub your chain with crumbs.°
A stoup of wine, Maria!

MALVOLIO Mistress Mary, if you prized my lady's favor at anything more than contempt, you would not give means° for
this uncivil rule. She shall know of it, by this hand.   *Exit.* 110

MARIA Go shake your ears.°

SIR ANDREW 'Twere as good a deed as to drink when a man's
ahungry,° to challenge him in the field,° and then to break
promise with him, and make a fool of him.

SIR TOBY Do't, knight: I'll write thee a challenge; or I'll deliver   115
thy indignation to him by word of mouth.

MARIA Sweet Sir Toby, be patient for tonight. Since the youth
of the count's was today with my lady, she is much out of
quiet. For Monsieur Malvolio, let me alone with him. If I do
not gull° him into a nayword,° and make him a common   120
recreation,° do not think I have wit enough to lie straight in
my bed. I know I can do it.

SIR TOBY Possess° us, possess us; tell us something of him.

MARIA Marry sir, sometimes he is a kind of Puritan.

SIR ANDREW O, if I thought that, I'd beat him like a dog.   125

SIR TOBY What, for being a Puritan? Thy exquisite° reason, dear
knight.

SIR ANDREW I have no exquisite reason for't, but I have reason
good enough.   129

MARIA The devil a Puritan that he is, or anything constantly but
a time-pleaser;° an affectioned° ass, that cons state without

(mother of Virgin Mary)
(used to spice ale)

101-5 Challenged by Feste's "dare," Sir Toby puts Malvolio in his (socially inferior) place and then claims the freedom of feasting and holiday (as at Twelfth Night; see line 74). Feste joins in to say that this must include freedom of speech too.

polish your chain of office /
    mind your own business

i.e., provide the liquor

please yourself (proverbial)

(for *thirsty*: perverting a
    proverb)   field of battle

106-15 Sir Toby makes the last attack on Malvolio directly, probably face to face, and again he alludes to the steward's inferior employment and social status. Then he turns away to call for wine, bringing Maria back into focus. Malvolio does not answer him but, before leaving, threatens Maria with the dire consequences of her complicity in the disorder.

After facing ridicule with silence since line 96, Malvolio makes a self-assured exit. Maria mocks him only as he is leaving; and only then does Sir Andrew propose a cowardly action that would disgrace his own knighthood. But Malvolio's dignity is also absurd at such a time: Laurence Olivier, in the role, raised his hand on "by this hand!" so that his underpants fell down from beneath a nightshirt.

Feste plays no further part in the scene; usually he falls asleep or sits apart absorbed in his melancholy. Formerly it was traditional for Feste to follow Malvolio offstage, "mocking him" (Kemble ed., 1811)

trick   byword
laughingstock

give us the facts

117-55 Maria and the two knights now huddle together to plot their revenge. Maria takes her time to get to the nub of her plot. By line 137, she has Sir Toby's complete attention, which may well be her chief purpose (see line 158); she says only enough to let him seem to think of the plot for himself (see lines 146-47). In keeping with her liveliness throughout the play, she leaves quickly as soon as they are agreed.

farfetched, precise (Andrew
    interprets this to mean
    excellent, line 128)

yes-man   affected

book° and utters it by great swaths;° the best persuaded° of
himself; so crammed, as he thinks, with excellencies, that it is
his grounds° of faith that all that look on him love him: and
on that vice in him will my revenge find notable cause to   135
work.

SIR TOBY   What wilt thou do?

MARIA   I will drop in his way some obscure epistles of love,
wherein by the color of his beard, the shape of his leg. the
manner of his gait, the expressure° of his eye, forehead, and   140
complexion, he shall find himself most feelingly° personated.
I can write very like my lady your niece; on a forgotten matter we can hardly make distinction of our hands.

SIR TOBY   Excellent! I smell a device.

SIR ANDREW   I have't in my nose too.   145

SIR TOBY   He shall think by the letters that thou wilt drop that
they come from my niece, and that she's in love with him.

MARIA   My purpose is indeed a horse of that color.°

SIR ANDREW   And your horse now would make him an ass.

MARIA   Ass, I doubt not.   150

SIR ANDREW   O 'twill be admirable.

MARIA   Sport royal, I warrant you. I know my physic will work
with him. I will plant you two, and let the fool make a third,
where he shall find the letter. Observe his construction of it.
For this night, to bed, and dream on the event.° Farewell.   155
                                                        Exit.

SIR TOBY   Good night, Penthesilia.°

SIR ANDREW   Before me,° she's a good wench.

SIR TOBY   She's a beagle true-bred, and one that adores me. What
o' that?

SIR ANDREW   I was adored once too.   160

SIR TOBY   Let's to bed, knight.—Thou hadst need send for more
money.

memorizes high toned etiquette
heaps   assured

basis

expression*

understandingly, appropriately

something of that sort

158-59   A crux for the interpretation of Sir Toby: the degree of his feeling for Maria is expressed by reference to a hunting dog, but "adores" is an especially potent word in this play (see commentary on II.i.38-42). "What o' that?" can suggest either an instinctive avoidance of too demanding a personal relationship or a deeper defeatism. Much depends on how Maria balances her control over the knight with a display of affection for him.

outcome

(queen of warlike Amazons)

I swear, with myself as witness

160   This line is justly famous, both for comedy and sentiment. It is the most absurd of Sir Andrew's echoes of Sir Toby, for he is always merely paraphrasing his mentor and master, but, coming at the climax of the excitement of Maria's plotting, its anticlimactic and pathetic vagueness (and no doubt falsehood) draws attention to Sir Andrew himself. Its self-assertion may achieve nothing to Sir Andrew's immediate purpose; Sir Toby, ready for bed, can either ignore it or reply by offering a weary good comradeship.

161-68   Between Sir Toby's resolve to go to bed and his decision that it is too late, the two knights touch on financial and other realities. Ironies should be marked in performance: Sir Andrew worries that Sir Toby might not trust him, not *vice versa*; Toby is using Andrew to get money, yet concludes by insisting on his company.

     The scene's ending can be slow and painfully muddled, or more broadly comic. Sometimes, by

SIR ANDREW   If I cannot recover° your niece, I am a foul way out.°

SIR TOBY   Send for money, knight; if thou hast her not i' th'
end, call me Cut.°   165

SIR ANDREW   If I do not, never trust me, take it how you will.

SIR TOBY   Come, come; I'll go burn some sack;° 'tis too late to go
to bed now. Come knight; come knight.   *Exeunt*

Scene iv   *Enter* DUKE, VIOLA, CURIO, *and others.*

DUKE   Give me some music. Now good morrow, friends.
Now good Cesario, but that piece of song,
That old and antic° song we heard last night:
Methought it did relieve my passion° much,
More than light airs, and recollected° terms°   5
Of these most brisk and giddy-paced times.
Come, but one verse.

CURIO   He is not here, so please your lordship, that should sing it.

DUKE   Who was it?

CURIO   Feste the jester, my lord; a fool that the Lady Olivia's   10
father took much delight in. He is about the house.

DUKE   Seek him out, and play the tune the while.
                              [*Exit* CURIO.] *Music plays.*
Come hither, boy. If ever thou shalt love,
In the sweet pangs of it, remember me;
For such as I am, all true lovers are,   15
Unstaid and skittish in all motions° else,
Save in the constant image of the creature
That is beloved. How dost thou like this tune?

VIOLA   It gives a very echo to the seat
Where Love is throned.°

DUKE   Thou dost speak masterly.   20
My life upon't, young though thou art, thine eye

obtain   out of pocket

cart horse (term of abuse)

the last line, Toby discovers that his companion is asleep and has to wake him or leave him; or Sir Andrew can find a new lease on life, repeatedly calling Toby "Cut" as he leaves the stage (as in Kemble ed., 1811).

heat and spice (and drink)
   some Spanish wine

<u>Scene iv</u>

1   In this scene, Viola can seem to taunt Orsino playfully about his love and yet suffer with him too, and on account of her own feelings. In Jonathan Miller's production at the Arts, Cambridge, in 1969, she and Orsino talked "quietly to each other of their feelings, he with a stupid male conceit, she with a desperate and disguised tenderness"; the scene became "a haunting commentary on the deceits by which men hide themselves from women yet reveal themselves to men" (*New Statesman* , 3 October).

strange

suffering

farfetched (?)*   expressions

In Peter Hall's productions at Stratford in 1958 and 1960, the whole play was "saturated with a sense of life's brevity," and when Orsino remarked that "women are as roses" that fall at the "very hour" of their flowering, Dorothy Tutin's "And so they are" was "sighed out in so resigned a way that it captured the whole Ronsardian flavor of the passage" (*Scotsman*, 19 May 1960).

Strong feelings and contrary purposes give energy to this scene while the dialogue's sustained syntax, imagery, and metrical pattern in the longer speeches give it dramatic power. Moments of sharp recognition and of feeling too deep or private for words ensure its intensity. The whole needs to be judged carefully in performance.

1-13   The first entry repeats the visual image of l.i: Orsino is "melancholy" (see line 70), forgetful (not knowing who sang the song), changeable (showing no pleasure after the song; contrast l.i.4-7). But now no one suggests alternative pastimes; even Feste enters silently (see line 40). A further contrast is that Viola is present and tries to avoid contact: she does not answer when spoken to (at lines 2 and 13, and perhaps 7); and may even move away since, at line 13, Orsino has to call her to him.

impulses, emotions

The time is probably early morning (see "good morro," line 1), contrasting with the previous scene.

it exactly reflects what the
   heart says

18-37   Viola, whose silence has been marked, is asked a seemingly simple question and in answering (lines 19-20) betrays, with a few, fanciful words, an

Hath stayed upon some favor° that it loves;
Hath it not, boy?

VIOLA   A little by your favor.°

DUKE   What kind of woman is't?

VIOLA   Of your complexion.°

DUKE   She is not worth thee then. What years, i' faith?   25

VIOLA   About your years, my lord

DUKE   Too old, by heaven. Let still° the woman take
An elder than herself; so wears° she to him,
So sways she level° in her husband's heart;
For, boy, however we do praise ourselves,   30
Our fancies° are more giddy and unfirm,°
More longing, wavering, sooner lost and worn,°
Than women's are.

VIOLA   I think it well, my lord.

DUKE   Then let thy love be younger than thyself,
Or thy affection cannot hold the bent;°   35
For women are as roses, whose fair flow'r
Being once displayed, doth fall that very hour.

VIOLA   And so they are; alas, that they are so—
To die, even when they to perfection grow.

Enter CURIO *and* CLOWN.

DUKE   O fellow, come, the song we had last night.   40
Mark it Cesario, it is old and plain:
The spinsters° and the knitters in the sun,
And the free° maids that weave their thread with bones,°
Do use to chant it. It is silly sooth,°
And dallies° with the innocence of love,   45
Like the old age.°

CLOWN   Are you ready sir?

DUKE   I prithee sing.   *Music.*

appearance

permission

temperament, appearance

always

adapts

she maintains a steady course

loves   fickle

forgotten

be constant in direction/stay
   at full power (like a bent
   bow)

spinners

carefree   bone bobbins

simple truth

plays/lingers

the Golden Age of classical
   legend

assurance that catches Orsino's attention. He is surprised and compliments his "boy." He probably laughs at the incongruity as he teases Cesario about his manhood, and so Viola is drawn into speaking about her master, protected at first by playfulness.

For most of the following dialogue, Viola is probably closer to Orsino than before and perhaps sitting at his feet, looking away at the musicians or into the distance. In their instinctive game, the Duke makes all the overt moves; Viola is more hesitant because if their eyes meet for more than a moment, she will experience real feeling and be in danger of betraying it. A half-line (26) suggests a pause for such a moment of recognition and subsequent avoidance.

38-39 Viola has recognized Orsino's familiar proverb and repeats it in harsher terms, betraying something of her own feelings. A mutual silence seems required here, for neither continues the thought. The entrance of Feste to stand watching, unusually silent, would both emphasize and help to hold such a silence by his wordless reaction to it.

CLOWN [*Sings.*] Come away, come away, death,
    And in sad cypress° let me be laid.   50
   Fly away, fly away, breath;
   I am slain by a fair cruel maid.
     My shroud of white, stuck all with yew,
      O prepare it.
     My part° of death, no one so true 55
      Did share it.
  Not a flower, not a flower sweet,
   On my black coffin let there be strewn;
  Not a friend, not a friend greet
   My poor corpse, where my bones shall be
       thrown.   60
     A thousand thousand sighs to save,
      Lay me, O where
    Sad true lover never find my grave,
     To weep there.

DUKE There's for thy pains.   65

CLOWN No pains, sir: I take pleasure in singing, sir.

DUKE I'll pay thy pleasure then.

CLOWN Truly sir, and pleasure will be paid,° one time or another.

DUKE Give me now leave to leave thee.

CLOWN Now the melancholy god° protect thee, and the tailor 70
make thy doublet of changeable taffeta,° for thy mind is a
very opal.° I would have men of such constancy put to sea,
that their business might be everything, and their intent°
everywhere; for that's it, that always makes a good voyage
of nothing. Farewell.   *Exit* 75

DUKE Let all the rest give place.°
        [*Exeunt* CURIO *and* ATTENDANTS.]
      Once more Cesario,
Get thee to yond same sovereign cruelty.
Tell her my love, more noble than the world,
Prizes not quantity of dirty lands:
The parts° that fortune hath bestowed upon her, 80
Tell her I hold as giddily as fortune,
But 'tis that miracle and queen of gems°

coffin of cypress wood

49-65   The song that Orsino couples with carefree innocence of an imaginary and golden age (see lines 44-46) is, in fact, an ornate and delicate evocation of despair, isolation, and death. The music that has been playing (perhaps since line 12) has prepared the audience for its mood, and so it is Orsino's introduction that will seem incongruous, not the song itself. Viola has evoked a mood in Orsino at variance with the song's melancholy at the beginning of the scene; he says nothing to express pleasure in the song and dismisses Feste briefly (65). Soon he dismisses all attendants except Cesario (see line 76) and then reasserts himself.

act/portion

(proverbially, pleasure is paid for with pain)

Saturn

shot silk

(gem, changing color according to light)

destination/desire

70-75   Unlike Orsino's servants, Feste does not obey immediately or silently. He makes explicit a criticism that may have been implied in his first question (line 47) and finishes with a mockingly false compliment and an abrupt "Farewell."

withdraw

gifts

i.e., Olivia's beauty

That nature pranks her in,° attracts my soul.

VIOLA   But if she cannot love you, sir?

DUKE   I cannot be so answered.

VIOLA   Sooth,° but you must.   85
Say that some lady, as perhaps there is,
Hath for your love as great a pang of heart
As you have for Olivia. You cannot love her;
You tell her so. Must she not then be answered?

DUKE   There is no woman's sides   90
Can bide° the beating of so strong a passion
As love doth give my heart; no woman's heart
So big, to hold so much: they lack retention.°
Alas, their love may be called appetite,
No motion° of the liver° but the palate,   95
That suffer surfeit, cloyment° and revolt;°
But mine is all as hungry as the sea,
And can digest as much. Make no compare
Between that love a woman can bear me,
And that I owe Olivia.

VIOLA   Ay, but I know—   100

DUKE   What dost thou know?

VIOLA   Too well what love women to men may owe.
In faith, they are as true of heart as we.
My father had a daughter loved a man
As it might be perhaps, were I a woman,   105
I should your lordship.

DUKE   And what's her history?

VIOLA   A blank, my lord. She never told her love,
But let concealment, like a worm i' th' bud,
Feed on her damask° cheek. She pined in thought,
And with a green and yellow melancholy,   110
She sat like Patience on a monument,
Smiling at grief. Was not this love indeed?
We men may say more, swear more, but indeed
Our shows are more than will;° for still we prove
Much in our vows, but little in our love.   115

adorns her with

truly

85-100 For the first time, Orsino is directly contradicted (line 85). He does not answer, but Viola follows with argument. She has stepped closer to him, metaphorically and, perhaps, literally.

Orsino's half-line (90) suggests that he pauses before replying in flat contradiction to his earlier advice (see lines 30-33); he may well move away from Viola in self-assertion.

endure

ability to retain*

stirring   (seat of passion)
satiety*   revulsion

100-106 For the third time, Viola's heartfelt words arrest Orsino's attention but now, after a pause (see the half-line 101), Viola risks speaking further under a more transparent disguise. The rhythms of lines 103-06 invite careful, deliberate speaking of her very simple words.

107-19 On Orsino's encouragement (see line 106), Viola dares to describe herself until, at the middle or end of line 112, she has to break off and resume Cesario's role, possibly with some mannish movement to emphasize what she says and help herself back into a fuller deception.

rose-colored

When Orsino's inquiry persists (line 116), Viola is forced back to speak of herself; she hides behind a riddle and, then, in ambiguity. With "and yet I know not" she can allude to her hope for Sebastian's life or to her own helplessness in love. At this point, she briskly directs attention back to Olivia (see line 119), as if needing to escape from her own thoughts.

we pretend to more than the
sexual drive we feel

DUKE   But died thy sister of her love, my boy?

VIOLA   I am all the daughters of my father's house,
And all the brothers too:—and yet I know not.
Sir, shall I to this lady?

DUKE   Ay, that's the theme.
To her in haste: give her this jewel; say,   120
My love can give no place,° bide no denay°   *Exeunt.*

Scene v   *Enter* SIR TOBY, SIR ANDREW, *and* FABIAN.

SIR TOBY   Come thy ways, Signior Fabian.

FABIAN   Nay I'll come. If I lose a scruple° of this sport, let me
be boiled° to death with melancholy.

SIR TOBY   Wouldst thou not be glad to have the niggardly ras-
cally sheep-biter° come by some notable shame?   5

FABIAN   I would exult, man. You know he brought me out o'
favor with my lady about a bearbaiting here.

SIR TOBY   To anger him we'll have the bear again, and we will
fool him black and blue.—Shall we not Sir Andrew?

SIR ANDREW   And we do not, it is pity of our lives.   10

Enter MARIA.

SIR TOBY   Here comes the little villain. How now, my metal of
India?°

MARIA   Get ye all three into the box tree: Malvolio's coming
down this walk. He has been yonder i' the sun practicing
behavior° to his own shadow this half hour. Observe him,   15
for the love of mockery; for I know this letter will make a
contemplative idiot of him. Close,° in the name of jesting!
[*The others hide.*] Lie thou there: [*Throws down a letter.*] for
here comes the trout, that must be caught with tickling.° *Exit.*

119-21 The short, emphatic phrases break the intimate mood. But as the two almost touch in exchanging the "jewel," there can be another swift change of consciousness and the final line gain urgency by an unspoken recognition of the feeling that is growing between them.

cannot yield   denial

The *Exeunt* can be played several ways: either Viola can hurry off leaving Orsino to new sensations; or Orsino can leave first and Viola go regretfully in an opposite direction; or, at exactly the same pace and simultaneously, each can run off or leave very slowly, in opposite directions. The conclusion of the scene should be a sensitive response to whatever degree of mutual affection has been expressed earlier: it a delicate moment which must always be played by ear at each new performance.

Scene v

smallest part
(pun on *bile,* supposed cause of *cold* melancholy)

i.e., sneaky dog

1-10 Sir Toby enters calling a servant by the title of a gentleman. The audience will have expected Feste to "make a third" in the plot (see II.iii.153), but Shakespeare's introduction of Fabian in his place serves several dramatic purposes: 1) it brings more of Olivia's household into focus and shows Sir Toby's dependence on such company; 2) it provides a restraint (and a more detached view) to this "letter scene", just as "drunk scenes" are the better for one sober man; 3) Fabian's harsh, strained images (and often his longer, less emphatic rhythms) provide contrasts of sentiment and sound—he is a compact, sour, tenacious man who is at length roused to short-lived excitement.

i.e., golden girl

elegance, poise

be still

stroking (i.e., flattery)

13 Three into one "box tree" will hardly fit. This may well provide part of the visual humor, especially as the two knights are several times impelled to rush out and "beat" (29) or "pistol" (33) the "scab" (68). But usually several trees are provided, and the eavesdroppers move from one to another as they seek a better view of Malvolio and as they threaten him and try to restrain themselves.

Enter MALVOLIO.

MALVOLIO   'Tis but fortune; all is fortune. Maria once told me   20
she did affect° me, and I have heard herself come thus
near, that, should she fancy,° it should be one of my complexion. Besides she uses me with a more exalted respect
than anyone else that follows° her. What should I think
on't?   25

SIR TOBY   Here's an overweening rogue.

FABIAN   O peace! Contemplation makes a rare turkey cock of
him; how he jets° under his advanced° plumes!

SIR ANDREW   'Slight,° I could so beat the rogue.

SIR TOBY   Peace, I say.   30

MALVOLIO   To be Count Malvolio.

SIR TOBY   Ah rogue!

SIR ANDREW   Pistol him, pistol him.

SIR TOBY   Peace, peace.

MALVOLIO   There is example for't: the Lady of the Strachy°   35
married the yeoman of the wardrobe.

SIR ANDREW   Fie on him, Jezebel!°

FABIAN   O peace! Now he's deeply in: look how imagination
blows° him.

MALVOLIO   Having been three months married to her, sitting   40
in my state . . .°

SIR TOBY   O for a stonebow,° to hit him in the eye!

MALVOLIO   Calling my officers about me, in my branched°
velvet gown . . . having come from a daybed, where I have
left Olivia sleeping   45

SIR TOBY   Fire and brimstone!°

FABIAN   O peace, peace!

MALVOLIO   And then to have the humor of state:° and after a de-
mure travel of regard° . . . telling them I know my place, as I

have a liking for

fall in love

serves

20ff. Fabian's descriptions (see lines 27-28, 38-39) imply that when Malvolio is silent he is responding physically to his own thoughts, as if undertaking a comically ambitious rehearsal, trying several gestures to achieve each exalted effect that he considers appropriate to "Count Malvolio" (31). Maria says he has been doing this for half-an-hour already (see lines 14-15). He is carried away by his fantasies, physically as well as mentally, until his performance is total and isolates him from others. The letter gives exterior evidence that his fantasy has become reality and now, with this in hand, he can admit that he has suffered previously through indulging his exotic imagination in private (see lines 146-47) when in reality his achievement was mundane.

struts   uplifted

by God's light

30, 34 Some editors re-assign these lines to Fabian, but there may well be an intended joke when, a little later, Fabian has to take over command of the situation and, with increasing difficulty, restrain the enraged knight as Malvolio speaks of marriage to Olivia (see lines 38, 47, 53, 59-60, which grow in force).

(uncertain topical allusion)

(type of wicked, impudent
    woman; see *I Kings* xvi.29 ff.)

31, 40-45 At Hartford Stage in 1985, Benjamin Stewart's Malvolio was full of himself: "'To be,' he says, and pauses as if to Hamletize, then glows, as he finishes the sentence, 'Count Malvolio!'" (*New York Times,* 11 October, 1985).

Malvolio is in love, not with Olivia, but with himself. He gets his satisfaction by dismissing Olivia from his thoughts and being mindful of his own appearance and clothes.

At first, Malvolio walks to and fro while the others hide, but at lines 40-41 he probably sits, while the others move behind and around him.

puffs up/betrays

chair of state

crossbow that shoots stones

embroidered

(flames and sulfur of hell)

a mind to be the great man
i.e., after looking around
    gravely (at his officers)

would they should do theirs . . . to ask for my kinsman   50
Toby . . . .

SIR TOBY   Bolts and shackles!

FABIAN   O peace, peace, peace, now, now!

MALVOLIO   Seven of my people, with an obedient start,
make out for° him: I frown the while, and perchance wind   55
up my watch, or play with my—some rich jewel . . . Toby
approaches; curtsies° there to me . . . .

SIR TOBY   Shall this fellow live?

FABIAN   Though our silence be drawn from us with cars,° yet
peace.   60

MALVOLIO   I extend my hand to him thus . . . quenching my
familiar smile with an austere regard of control° . . . .

SIR TOBY   And does not Toby take° you a blow o' the lips then?

MALVOLIO   Saying, "Cousin Toby, my fortunes having cast me
on your niece, give me this prerogative of speech . . ."   65

SIR TOBY   What, what?

MALVOLIO   "You must amend your drunkenness."

SIR TOBY   Out, scab!

FABIAN   Nay patience, or we break the sinews of our plot.

MALVOLIO   "Besides, you waste the treasure of your time   70
with a foolish knight . . ."

SIR ANDREW   That's me, I warrant you.

MALVOLIO   "One Sir Andrew."

SIR ANDREW   I knew 'twas I, for many do call me fool.

MALVOLIO   What employment have we here?   75

[*Takes up the letter.*]

FABIAN   Now is the woodcock° near the gin.°

SIR TOBY   O peace! and the spirit of humors° intimate reading
aloud to him!

i.e., go to fetch

bows

by torture (a victim was tied to
two chariots, driven in
opposite directions)

look of authority

give

(proverbially stupid bird)
trap
whims

56   Most Malvolios obviously stop themselves
from saying "my chain" (of office), substituting a more
count-like bauble. His "thus" at line 61 shows he is
still conscious that he is only pretending to be Count
Malvolio.

72-78   Sir Andrew should here come further out of
hiding than Sir Toby: he is positively pleased to be
included (see line 72) and seems to escape the
attention of Fabian (who is probably still strenuously
engaged with Sir Toby). At line 74, he is about to give
the eavesdroppers away when the plot is saved by
Malvolio's sudden observation of the letter. Some
Fabians have rushed from cover to push the letter
under Malvolio's nose; others manage to kick it in
front of him at the last moment, as one hand holds
Toby and the other Andrew.
     Once Malvolio has the letter, even Sir
Toby calls for "peace."

MALVOLIO By my life, this is my lady's hand: these be her very
   C's, her U's, and her T's; and thus makes she her great P's.   80
   It is, in contempt of° question, her hand.

SIR ANDREW Her C's, her U's, and her T's? Why that?

MALVOLIO [*Reads.*] "To the unknown beloved, this, and my
   good wishes." Her very phrases! By your leave, wax.°
   Soft!°—and the impressure her Lucrece,° with which she   85
   uses to seal. 'Tis my lady: to whom should this be?

FABIAN This wins him, liver° and all.

MALVOLIO [*Reads.*] "Jove knows I love,
               But who?
            Lips, do not move;   90
               No man must know."
   "No man must know." What follows? The numbers° altered!
   "No man must know." If this should be thee, Malvolio?

SIR TOBY Marry, hang thee, brock!°

MALVOLIO [*Reads.*] "I may command where I adore,   95
            But silence, like a Lucrece knife,°
            With bloodless stroke my heart doth gore.
            M. O. A. I. doth sway my life."

FABIAN A fustian° riddle.

SIR TOBY Excellent wench, say I.   100

MALVOLIO "'M. O. A. I. doth sway my life." Nay, but first let
   me see, let me see, let me see.

FABIAN What dish o' poison has she dressed° him!

SIR TOBY And with what wing the staniel checks at it!°

MALVOLIO "I may command, where I adore." Why she may   105
   command me: I serve her; she is my lady. Why this is
   evident to any formal capacity.° There is no obstruction in
   this.—And the end: what should that alphabetical position
   portend? If I could make that resemble something in me!—
   Softly!—"M.O.A.I."   110

SIR TOBY O ay, make up that!—He is now at a cold scent.

beyond

(apologizing for breaking the seal)

wait   i.e., the seal depicts the chaste Lucrerce

(seat of passion)

meter

badger (proverbially, stinking)

(Lucrece stabbed herself after she was raped)

worthless / pretentious

prepared for

with what speed the hawk turns to it (and away from its true prey)

ordinary intelligence

80   "C" and "P" do not occur in the address that Malvolio reads out. Shakespeare may have been careless and chose these letters so that Sir Andrew may think Malvolio is being called "Cut" (see II.iii.165). Possibly Malvolio is not actually reading an inscription, but letting his imagination run away with him.

83-86   Malvolio does not hesitate to open the letter and only afterwards questions to whom it is addressed. A moment later he is reading aloud.
   For the rest of the scene, Malvolio alternates comically between reckless hope, determined ingenuity, baffled silence, and full, ecstatic belief.

92-93   The (strained) rhymes and the repeated wordplay on *no* and *know*, together with the *O's* in Malvolio's name, give plenty of opportunity for strange pronunciations that give comic displays of both puzzlement and growing elation.

99-102   The riddle has abruptly silenced Malvolio; he probably repeats it flatly at first (line 101) and then hurries to read the letter further. Turning back to the nagging riddle, he is several times baffled into silence, not speaking again until he has worked out something to his own satisfaction.
   Scholars disagree about what the initials mean. They could, possibly, be intentional nonsense, playing with letters in Malvolio's name (see lines 125-26) and tantalizing both him and the audience with something which sounds very obscure by being without any possible meaning. However, Elizabethans delighted in riddles, including some with more than one meaning, and also in anagrams. Among the more plausible solutions (*Connotations*, II.3, 1992) is that it is anagram of OMNIA, with the *N missing* and alluding to "OMNIA VINCAT AMOR" (Love conquers all).

105-10   Alliterative and pompous phrasing here and at lines 117-18 and 124-26 suggests that when Malvolio is puzzled he takes some comfort by speaking as a man of note: he maintains an earnest air of deliberation and good breeding, which heightens the comedy. Comments on his behavior suggest that he responds physically too (see lines 104, 112-13, 115-16).

FABIAN   Sowter will cry upon't for all this, though it be as rank
    as a fox .°

MALVOLIO   M . . . Malvolio. M. Why that begins my name.

FABIAN   Did not I say he would work it out? The cur is excel-   115
    lent at faults.°

MALVOLIO   M . . . But then there is no consonancy° in the sequel;
    that suffers under probation.° A. should follow, but O. does.

FABIAN   And "O"° shall end, I hope.

SIR TOBY   Ay, or I'll cudgel him, and make him cry "O!"   120

MALVOLIO   And then I. comes behind.

FABIAN   Ay,° and you had any eye° behind you, you might see
    more detraction at your heels than fortunes before you.

MALVOLIO   M. O. A. I. This simulation° is not as the former;—
    and yet to crush° this a little, it would bow to me, for every   125
    one of these letters are in my name. Soft, here follows prose!
    [*Reads.*] "If this fall into thy hand, revolve.° In my stars° I
    am above thee, but be not afraid of greatness: some are
    born great, some achieve greatness, and some have great-
    ness thrust upon 'em. Thy Fates open their hands; let thy   130
    blood and spirit embrace them; and to inure° thyself to
    what thou art like to be, cast thy humble slough,° and
    appear fresh. Be opposite with° a kinsman, surly with ser-
    vants. Let thy tongue tang° arguments of state; put thyself
    into the trick° of singularity.° She thus advises thee, that   135
    sighs for thee. Remember who commended thy yellow
    stockings, and wished to see thee ever cross-gartered.° I
    say, remember. Go to, thou art made, if thou desir'st to
    be so; if not, let me see thee a steward still, the fellow of
    servants, and not worthy to touch Fortune's fingers. Fare-   140
    well. She that would alter° services with thee,
                         THE FORTUNATE UNHAPPY."
    Daylight and champian° discovers° not more! This is open!
    I will be proud, I will read politic° authors, I will baffle°
    Sir Toby, I will wash off gross° acquaintance, I will be   145
    point-devise° the very man. I do not now fool myself, to
    let imagination jade° me, for every reason excites to this,

the stupid dog will yelp after
  the trail although it is obviously false

i.e., when off scent

agreement
falls down under examination

(i.e., omega, last letter in
  Greek alphabet, and in
  Malvolio)

(puns on *I*)

hidden meaning
strain

consider   fate

127-60   For the climax of Malvolio's "performance"
here, the onstage audience of eavesdroppers
is silent and should probably remain still or hidden; now
even Sir Toby does not react to insult (144-45).
Malvolio is so entranced that he does not interrupt his

accustom

outworn skin

stand up to

strike loud (as on a bell)

manner, dress   individual-
  ity / eccentricity

wearing garters above and
  below the knee, and crossed
  behind it

reading until the end of the letter's signature; holding
the audience's attention wholly, he can read with
increasingly bated breath or with an ever more difficult struggle to force back an expression of his growing pleasure; or he can immediately enact all the various injunctions of the letter.

exchange

open country   reveals
political   disgrace
coarse
precisely
misuse, befool

143-54   The letter finished, Malvolio bursts out in
delight and, in his imagination, hurries to anticipate
all the promised ecstasy. Speed and excitement are
obvious in the repeated "I will" and "she did," and are
in sharp contrast to his usual grave and deliberate
pace of which a few touches may still remain. For
Malvolio, the scene has now moved into the world of

that my lady loves me. She did commend my yellow stockings of late, she did praise my leg being cross-gartered: 149
and in this she manifests herself to my love, and with a kind
of injunction drives me to these habits° of her liking.—I
thank my stars, I am happy! I will be strange,° stout,° in
yellow stockings, and cross-gartered, even with the swift-
ness of putting on. Jove,° and my stars be praised!—Here is
yet apostscript: [*Reads.*] "Thou canst not choose but know   155
who I am. If thou entertainest° my love, let it appear in thy
smiling; thy smiles become thee well. Therefore in my
presence still smile, dear my sweet, I prithee." Jove, I thank
thee. I will smile; I will do everything that thou wilt have
me.   *Exit.*   160

FABIAN   I will not give my part of this sport for a pension of
thousands to be paid from the Sophy.°

SIR TOBY   I could marry this wench for this device.

SIR ANDREW   So could I too.

SIR TOBY   And ask no other dowry with her, but such another   165
jest.

Enter MARIA.

SIR ANDREW   Nor I neither.

FABIAN   Here comes my noble gull-catcher.

SIR TOBY   Wilt thou set thy foot o' my neck?

SIR ANDREW   Or o' mine either?   170

SIR TOBY   Shall I play° my freedom at tray-trip,° and become
thy bondslave?

SIR ANDREW   I' faith, or I either?

SIR TOBY   Why, thou hast put him in such a dream, that when
the image of it leaves him he must run mad.   175

MARIA   Nay but say true, does it work upon him?

SIR TOBY   Like aqua vitae° with a midwife.

MARIA   If you will then see the fruits of the sport, mark his first

his dreams and he believes it is for real.

this dress

remarkable, aloof   proud

(an original *God* may have
  been censored)

return

154-55   Malvolio is alert enough in his growing
excitement to spot the postscript; perhaps he has
sneaked another quick look at the letter for the confirmation that he still secretly needs.

159-60   Laurence Olivier, as Malvolio, "winds up
the scene with an inimitable piece of by-play in which
the grave steward, after several wry attempts to
smile into a mirror, achieves a satisfied asinine grin"
(Times, 22 April, 1955). Malvolio now takes his
orders from Jove.

Shah of Persia

163   Sir Toby is said to have married Maria
somewhere offstage by the end of the play (see
V.i.348), so this could be a moment of self-recogni-
tion, amid the laughter and satisfaction following
Malvolio's enraptured exit.

167-87   Maria, once more entering quickly on cue,
is unable to say a word as the two knights jostle
around her; they are so elated that she has to get
them to confirm that they are not fooling (see line
176). She leaves the suggestion of marriage (lines
171-2) unanswered.

Maria then takes everyone's attention by
proposing the next occasion for mocking Malvolio;
this time it will involve Olivia directly and, therefore,
be more public and more dangerous for their victim.
So she has them following her offstage without
debate. Sir Toby may well exit arm-in-arm with her or
hustling her on, or even lifting her aloft like a con-
queror. (In view of "wren", III.ii.56, the part is often
cast with an actress who is diminutive and light; originally, she would have been played by a boy, perhaps the smaller one who also played Celia to the
taller Rosalind in *As You Like It* or Hermia to Helena
in *The Dream*). Sir Andrew will be left standing and
there may be a short pause before he follows on
behind (see line 187).

risk   (a dice game)

hard liquor

approach before my lady: he will come to her in yellow
stockings, and 'tis a color she abhors, and cross-gartered,   180
a fashion she detests; and he will smile upon her, which
will now be so unsuitable to her disposition, being addicted
to a melancholy as she is, that it cannot but turn him into a
notable contempt. If you will see it, follow me.

Sɪʀ Toʙy   To the gates of Tartar,° thou most excellent devil of   185
wit.

Sɪʀ Aɴᴅʀᴇᴡ   I'll make one° too.   *Exeunt.*

Tartarus (deepest hell)

be there

ACT III

Scene i   *Enter* VIOLA *and* CLOWN [*with a tabor*].

VIOLA   Save thee, friend, and thy music. Dost thou live by° thy
tabor?°

CLOWN   No sir, I live by° the church.

VIOLA   Art thou a churchman?

CLOWN   No such matter, sir; I do live by the church; for I do live   5
at my house, and my house doth stand by the church.

VIOLA   So thou mayst say, the king lies by° a beggar, if a beggar
dwell near him; or the church stands by° thy tabor, if thy
tabor stand by the church.

CLOWN   You have said sir. To see this age! A sentence° is but a   10
chev'ril° glove to a good wit: how quickly the wrong side
may be turned outward!

VIOLA   Nay that's certain: they that dally° nicely° with words,
may quickly make them wanton.°

CLOWN   I would therefore my sister had had no name, sir.   15

VIOLA   Why, man?

CLOWN   Why sir, her name's a word, and to dally with that word,
might make my sister wanton. But indeed words are very
rascals, since bonds disgraced them.°

VIOLA   Thy reason, man?   20

CLOWN   Troth sir, I can yield you none without words, and words
are grown so false, I am loath to prove reason with them.

VIOLA   I warrant thou art a merry fellow, and car'st for nothing.

Act III. Scene i

by means of
small drum

beside

dwells near / has sex with
is near / upholds

maxim
soft, pliable leather

play / flirt   subtly
capricious / unchaste

1   If the play is performed without intervals (as in Elizabethan days), Feste can enter in time to watch Sir Toby, Sir Andrew, and Fabian follow their sport like fools at the end of the previous scene; he could accompany their departure on his "tabor" or drum (2). So Viola would encounter Feste when he is seemingly lost in his own thoughts.

Viola has heard Feste speak up to Orsino, but she takes the lead in questions and wordplay. However, Feste's talk of the dangers of names to his "sister" (15-19) causes her to play into his hands and then to change the subject (see line 23); perhaps she senses that this is an encounter with someone as quick witted as herself. Many Violas take Feste's words as a direct warning about the dangers of disguise, the fool having sensed her make-believe— besides she had recently invented a sister as a cover; see II.iv.104 ff.

i.e., since bonds have been
    needed to guarantee them

23-38   Viola has turned the talk towards Feste, but he still talks about her and this is repeated two

CLOWN   Not so sir; I do care for something; but in my conscience
sir, I do not care for you. If that be to care for nothing sir, I   25
would it would make you invisible.

VIOLA   Art not thou the Lady Olivia's fool?

CLOWN   No indeed sir. The Lady Olivia has no folly: she will keep
no fool sir, till she be married; and fools are as like husbands
as pilchards are to herrings—the husband's the bigger. I am   30
indeed not her fool, but her corrupter of words.

VIOLA   I saw thee late at the Count Orsino's.

CLOWN   Foolery, sir, does walk about the orb° like the sun; it
shines everywhere. I would be sorry sir, but° the fool should
be as oft with your master as with my mistress. I think I saw   35
your wisdom° there.

VIOLA   Nay, and thou pass upon° me, I'll no more with thee.
Hold, there's expenses for thee.   [*Gives a coin.*]

CLOWN   Now Jove, in his next commodity° of hair, send thee a
beard.   40

VIOLA   By my troth, I'll tell thee, I am almost sick for one,
though I would not have it grow on my chin.—Is thy lady
within?

CLOWN   Would not a pair of these° have bred, sir?

VIOLA   Yes, being kept together, and put to use.°   45

CLOWN   I would play Lord Pandarus° of Phrygia sir, to bring a
Cressida to this Troilus.

VIOLA   I understand you sir; [*Gives another coin.*] 'tis well begged.

CLOWN   The matter, I hope, is not great sir, begging but a beggar: Cressida was a beggar.° My lady is within, sir. I will   50
conster° to them whence you come: who you are, and what
you would, are out of my welkin;° I might say "element,"
but the word is overworn.°   *Exit.*

VIOLA   This fellow is wise enough to play the fool,
And to do that well craves° a kind of wit.°   55
He must observe their mood on whom he jests,
The quality of persons, and the time;

more times, until she gives him some money. He touches on her appearance, her suit to Olivia, and her relationship to Orsino, but in each sally he also alludes to himself: he cares for "something" that he keeps hidden; he corrupts words; and he moves above and beyond other men, impersonally, "like the sun" (33). So the actor has both the cue and the means to suggest an inner melancholy, while sparring professionally with the seeming boy who had approached him so confidently.

Only a small part of this encounter is necessary for the play's narrative. Usually, much of it is cut in performance, with the excuse that the wordplay is too cumbersome and old-fashioned, and that, possibly, it was added to keep the clown in the actors' company in full employment. But if played so that it is, markedly, one in a series of intimate encounters between Feste and each of the main characters in turn (see commentary, I.v.23-26). This can help clarify the dramatic structure of the comedy as its action becomes more boisterous; by the end of the play, Feste has nothing more to do than stay on stage alone and sing to himself and the audience.

A further reason for playing this episode at its full length is that Viola's reaction to Feste's probing contrasts with that of other characters: she fights back more persistently and draws the fool into speaking more about himself; she also gets him to be useful in announcing her arrival. Left alone, she considers the wisdom of folly and seems to identify herself as a kind of "fool" in pursuit of love.

44-53 As Feste fools more money out of Viola, he is exercising a fool's prerogative. His farewell is often played as an assurance that he will not give Viola's game away: he pretends it is beyond him and doesn't wait for thanks. He may well leave laughing.

54-62 Feste has already suggested that Viola is a fool (see line 36), and she will soon confess herself to be one (see line 138). So here, speaking of wisdom rather than wordplay, she seems to see herself in Feste: her whole venture has depended on "wit"

---

world
but that

i.e., folly

make a (witty) thrust at

delivery

i.e., coins

usury / sexual intercourse

(the prototype of all pimps; see *Troilus*, III.ii.)

(she became a harlot, leper, and beggar)
explain
sky, sphere
stale

requires   intelligence

And like the haggard,° check at° every feather
That comes before his eye. This is a practice
As full of labor as a wise man's art: 60
For folly that he wisely shows, is fit;
But wise men, folly-fall'n,° quite taint their wit.°

Enter Sɪʀ Tᴏʙʏ *and* Sɪʀ Aɴᴅʀᴇw.

Sɪʀ Tᴏʙʏ   Save you, gentleman.

Vɪᴏʟᴀ   And you, sir.

Sɪʀ Aɴᴅʀᴇw   *Dieu vous garde, monsieur.*°   65

Vɪᴏʟᴀ   *Et vous aussi; votre serviteur.* °

Sɪʀ Aɴᴅʀᴇw   I hope, sir, you are, and I am yours.

Sɪʀ Tᴏʙʏ   Will you encounter° the house? My niece is desirous
you should enter, if your trade° be to her.

Vɪᴏʟᴀ   I am bound° to your niece, sir; I mean, she is the list° of   70
my voyage.

Sɪʀ Tᴏʙʏ   Taste° your legs sir, put them to motion.

Vɪᴏʟᴀ   My legs do better understand° me sir, than I understand
what you mean by bidding me taste my legs.

Sɪʀ Tᴏʙʏ   I mean, to go sir, to enter.   75

Vɪᴏʟᴀ   I will answer you with gait° and entrance. But we are
prevented.°

Enter Oʟɪᴠɪᴀ *and* Mᴀʀɪᴀ.

Most excellent accomplished lady, the heavens rain odors on
you.

Sɪʀ Aɴᴅʀᴇw   That youth's a rare courtier!—"Rain odors"!—well.   80

Vɪᴏʟᴀ   My matter hath no voice,° lady, but to your own most
pregnant° and vouchsafed° ear.

Sɪʀ Aɴᴅʀᴇw   "Odors," "pregnant," and "vouchsafed"!—I'll
get 'em all three all ready.

untrained hawk   fly after   and secrecy (see I.ii.62). The soliloquy probably ends with laughter at her own witlessness.

fallen into folly   spoil their
common sense

63-77   Sir Toby was last seen in pursuit of Malvolio, but Olivia has honored Cesario by sending her own kinsman as messenger: Sir Toby and Sir Andrew are on their best behavior, the former somewhat stiff with unfamiliar dignity but alive with the ironic realization that this is for the sake of a mere boy and servant.

God protect you, sir

And you also; your servant

Viola plays the fool, dallying nicely with words (see lines 13-19 above), in a way that mocks Sir Toby's portentousness (and her own). Sir Toby becomes progressively more blunt and direct, to which Viola replies with a brisk pun and then walks off: Sir Toby has been beaten at his own kind of mockery.

go to (affected speech)
course/business
directing my sail/obliged
extent/desire

try

stand under, support

going (pun on *gate*)
forestalled

78-85   Olivia enters impatiently, not having waited for her messenger to return. Yet seeing Cesario, she is tongue-tied, either comically or pathetically. Viola, assuming a flattering style, fills the gap; she probably bows elaborately. Sir Andrew had been dashed by Viola's ready French, but he returns to speech energized by outright admiration. His effusions prevent the audience from concentrating on Olivia's inability to speak, and so maintain the comic mood.

cannot be spoken
receptive*   condescending*

OLIVIA   Let the garden door be shut, and leave me to my hearing.
[*Exeunt* SIR TOBY, SIR ANDREW, *and* MARIA.] Give me your   86
hand, sir.

VIOLA   My duty, madam, and most humble service.

OLIVIA   What is your name?

VIOLA   Cesario is your servant's name, fair princess.   90

OLIVIA   My servant, sir? 'Twas never merry world
Since lowly feigning° was called compliment:
Y' are servant to the Count Orsino, youth.

VIOLA   And he is yours, and his must needs be yours:
Your servant's servant is your servant, madam.   95

OLIVIA   For him, I think not on him; for his thoughts,
Would they were blanks, rather than filled with me.

VIOLA   Madam, I come to whet your gentle thoughts
On his behalf.

OLIVIA   O by your leave, I pray you.
I bad you never speak again of him;   100
But would you undertake another suit,
I had rather hear you, to solicit° that,
Than music from the spheres.°

VIOLA   Dear lady—

OLIVIA   Give me leave, beseech you. I did send,
After the last enchantment you did here,   105
A ring in chase of you. So did I abuse°
Myself, my servant, and, I fear me, you.
Under your hard construction° must I sit,
To force that on you in a shameful cunning
Which you knew none of yours. What might you think?   110
Have you not set mine honor at the stake
And baited it with all th' unmuzzled thoughts
That tyrannous heart can think?°
To one of your receiving°
Enough is shown; a cypress,° not a bosom,   115
Hides my heart. So let me hear you speak.

VIOLA   I pity you.

humble pretense

86-116 Olivia, playing as safe as she is able, speaks first to her household. She may well wait for them all to be gone before speaking to Cesario, but then she ensures that she touches his hand (lines 86-87). Viola is affected by the intimacy, for she retreats from wordplay at first. Olivia then replies with more wordplay (see lines 91-92) and two broad hints which unsuccessfully attempt to draw from Cesario some expression of regard for her. Viola knows Olivia is in love with Cesario and so, in disguise as the page, plays firmly against her.

As Olivia moves from "pray" to "beseech" (99, 104), she puts her own feelings more directly into words. Faced with Viola's knowing avoidance, she has had to take charge, and this gives her dramatic strength. She takes the lead in the dialogue until she his forced to wait for a response. The verse irregularity of lines 113-14 suggests a pause here.

urge
(the celestial harmony, supposed to be caused by the
   movement of planets and
   stars)

wrong, disgrace

interpretation

i.e., the claims of honor are beset by those of love, like a
   bear at the stake
sensitivity*
veil of mourning

OLIVIA   That's a degree to love.

VIOLA   No, not a grize;° for 'tis a vulgar proof°
That very oft we pity enemies.

OLIVIA   Why then, methinks 'tis time to smile again.   120
O world, how apt the poor are to be proud!
If one should be a prey, how much the better
To fall before the lion than the wolf.   *Clock strikes.*
The clock upbraids me with the waste of time.
Be not afraid good youth, I will not have you,   125
And yet, when wit and youth is come to harvest°
Your wife is like to reap a proper° man.
There lies your way, due west.°

VIOLA   Then westward ho°!
Grace and good disposition° attend your ladyship.
You'll nothing madam, to my lord, by me?   130

OLIVIA   Stay!
I prithee tell me what thou think'st of me.

VIOLA   That you do think you are not what you are.°

OLIVIA   If I think so, I think the same of you.°

VIOLA   Then think you right: I am not what I am.   135

OLIVIA   I would you were as I would have you be.

VIOLA   Would it be better madam, than I am?
I wish it might, for now I am your fool.°

OLIVIA   [*Aside.*] O what a deal of scorn looks beautiful
In the contempt and anger of his lip.   140
A murd'rous guilt shows not itself more soon
Than love that would seem hid: love's night is noon.°—
Cesario, by the roses of the spring,
By maidhood,° honor, truth, and everything,
I love thee so, that maugre° all thy pride,   145
Nor wit, nor reason, can my passion hide.
Do not extort thy reasons from this clause,°
For that° I woo, thou therefore hast no cause;°
But rather reason thus, with reason fetter:
Love sought is good, but given unsought is better.   150

step   common experience

117-19   Viola's first response is a complete change, acknowledging much that she has tried to avoid saying. When Olivia seizes upon this hopefully, the exchange becomes more relaxed and Viola goes on to glance at her own feelings as a rival for Orsino's love. With comparatively little to say in this scene, Viola has opportunities to show, in contrast with Olivia's activity, the deep and unchanging source of her masquerade.

i.e., when you are mature

fine

(i.e., toward the setting sun)

(cry of London watermen
   ready to row up the Thames)

peace of mind

120-31   Olivia forces a smile at the repulse, regaining some dignity despite her thoughts of poverty and beasts of prey. She no longer addresses Viola, so probably moves away from her and then assumes a false airiness and benevolence. As Viola is about to go, Olivia's composure is broken and she cries out, simply, to hold Cesario back (131).

you (by loving a servant) are
   not being the lady you are

I, likewise, think you are the
   lord you are not

132-38   The one-line interchanges can be read as bantering wordplay, but Olivia's following recognition of "scorn," "contempt," and "anger" indicates that Viola is no longer patient. The confrontation becomes awkward and alive with deepest feeling; it shows important new facets of Viola's character as she reveals her passion, frustration, and willpower.

i..e., you are making a fool of
   me

i.e., love is plainly visible, even
   when hidden

virginity

in spite of

do not persuade yourself by
   what I have said
that because   interest (in
   her love)

139-50   Olivia turns away for her aside, but before Viola can leave the stage, she turns back again to speak Cesario's name for the first time and then to confess her love. Some Olivias kneel to Viola or take her hands; all must abandon pretense, affectation, and reserve. The four-line avowal (143-46) hinges on the simple words, "I love thee so." However, traces of critical self-awareness and insecurity may yet remain; certainly before Viola can reply, Olivia tries to forestall excuses.

VIOLA   By innocence I swear, and by my youth,
        I have one heart, one bosom, and one truth,°
        And that no woman has; nor never none
        Shall mistress be of it, save I alone.
        And so adieu, good madam. Never more   155
        Will I my master's tears to you deplore.

OLIVIA   Yet come again; for thou perhaps mayst move
        That heart, which now abhors, to like his love.   *Exeunt.*

Scene ii   *Enter* SIR TOBY, SIR ANDREW, *and* FABIAN.

SIR ANDREW   No, faith, I'll not stay a jot longer.

SIR TOBY   Thy reason, dear venom: give thy reason.

FABIAN   You must needs yield your reason, Sir Andrew.

SIR ANDREW   Marry, I saw your niece do more favors to the
        count's servingman than ever she bestowed upon me. I   5
        saw't i' th' orchard.

SIR TOBY   Did she see thee the while, old boy? Tell me that.

SIR ANDREW   As plain as I see you now.

FABIAN   This was a great argument° of love in her toward you.

SIR ANDREW   'Slight, will you make an ass o' me?   10

FABIAN   I will prove it legitimate° sir, upon the oaths of judgment
        and reason.°

SIR TOBY   And they have been grand-jurymen since before Noah
        was a sailor.°

FABIAN   She did show favor to the youth in your sight only to ex-   15
        asperate you, to awake your dormouse° valor, to put fire in
        your heart, and brimstone in your liver. You should then have
        accosted her, and with some excellent jests, fire-new from the
        mint, you should have banged the youth into dumbness. This   19
        was looked for at your hand, and this was balked.° The double

love, . . . affection, . . . devotion

151-58 Viola riddles partly to protect herself and partly to avoid downright lying. As she bids farewell and starts to go, Olivia, in three quick words, begs for a return and then follows this entreaty with a flattering bait that is belied by all her previous words and actions. To this Viola makes no reply and Olivia is now left alone, without further words; some actresses run weeping from the stage.

Scene ii

1-14 Sir Andrew, for the first time, enters ahead of the others; Sir Toby's "venom" suggests that he is furious. He will not answer Sir Toby directly, but only after Fabian's further persuasion. The two men probably position themselves one to each side of Sir Andrew, perhaps restraining him physically while they try to make him valiant by a brainwashing.

proof

genuine
(omitting third oath of truth)

(i.e., when God repented "he had made man on the earth")

sleepy

15-32 Fabian's show of expertise has silenced Sir Andrew's newfound common sense, and he continues to hold attention by suggesting a heroic role for the knight. Sir Andrew, as he often does, falls for a grand notion of himself. A good comic actor will, step by step, change from defeat and retreat, to reconsideration, and then to action. Sir Andrew says little, but he is the center of attention and by line 25 he is a new man.

avoided

gilt° of this opportunity you let time wash off, and you are now
sailed into the North of my lady's opinion,° where you will
hang like an icicle on a Dutchman's beard,° unless you do
redeem it by some laudable atempt, either of valor or policy.°

SIR ANDREW   And't be any way, it must be with valor; for policy   25
I hate. I had as lief be a Brownist° as a politician.

SIR TOBY   Why then, build me thy fortunes upon the basis of val-
or. Challenge me the count's youth to fight with him; hurt
him in eleven places. My niece shall take note of it, and assure
thyself there is no love-broker in the world can more prevail   30
in man's commendation with woman, than report of valor.

FABIAN   There is no way but this, Sir Andrew.

SIR ANDREW   Will either of you bear me a challenge to him?

SIR TOBY   Go, write it in a martial hand. Be curst° and brief; it is
no matter how witty,° so it be eloquent and full of invention.° 35
Taunt him with the license of ink;° if thou "thou'st"° him
some thrice, it shall not be amiss; and as many lies as will lie
in thy sheet of paper, although the sheet were big enough for
the bed of Ware° in England, set 'em down. Go about it. Let
there be.gall° enough in thy ink, though thou write with a   40
goose-pen,° no matter. About it!

SIR ANDREW   Where shall I find you?

SIR TOBY   We'll call thee at the cubiculo.° Go.   *Exit* SIR ANDREW.

FABIAN   This is a dear manikin° to you, Sir Toby.

SIR TOBY   I have been dear° to him, lad, some two thousand   45
strong or so.

FABIAN   We shall have a rare letter from him: but you'll not
deliver't?

SIR TOBY   Never trust me then; and by all means stir on the
youth to an answer. I think oxen and wainropes° cannot   50
hale° them together. For Andrew, if he were opened, and
you find so much blood in his liver as will clog the foot of a
flea, I'll eat the rest of th' anatomy.°

FABIAN   And his opposite,° the youth, bears in his visage no

plating of gold

into Olivia's cold disdain

(William Barentz sailed to the
   Arctic 1596-97)

stratagem

member of Puritan sect of
   Independents

33   Sir Andrew had first been guarded (see lines 25-26), but now he disdains to argue, speaking only to ask for assistance. In his own mind he is fully resolved and already the victor: in bearing, he will be transformed. Sir Toby can once again mock him to his face, without fear of discovery (see, especially, "goose-pen," lines 40-41).

virulent

intelligible   fabrication

(merely) written words
   (*thou* was used as mark of
   familiarity or contempt)

(famous bed, ten foot square)

ingredient of ink/bitterness

quill pen/pen belonging to a
   fool*

42-44   Although he is now resolved to fight, Sir Andrew is still reluctant to proceed further: Sir Toby has dismissed him three times and yet he is still on stage (see lines 34, 39, 41). His "Where shall I find you?" could suggest that he is still afraid of being on his own; but Sir Toby's fourth, and brief, "Go" is silently obeyed. A comic actor will take advantage of being the center of interest as Sir Andrew becomes solemnly absorbed in following the zany instructions; after his last hesitation he will leave the stage like an automaton. Fabian's "manikin" suggests some such exit—a clockwork soldier wound up to sudden, frenzied movement. Certainly the exit is a great contrast to his entry to the scene.

bed chamber (affected usage)

puppet

costly

wagon ropes

haul

corpse

opponent

great presage of cruelty.   55

Enter MARIA.

SIR TOBY   Look where the youngest wren° of nine comes.

MARIA   If you desire the spleen,° and will laugh yourselves into
stitches, follow me. Yond gull Malvolio is turned heathen, a
very renegado;° for there is no Christian that means to be
saved by believing rightly, can ever believe such impossible   60
passages of grossness.° He's in yellow stockings.

SIR TOBY   And cross-gartered?

MARIA   Most villainously; like a pedant° that keeps a school i' th'
church. I have dogged him like his murderer. He does obey
every point of the letter that I dropped to betray him. He does   65
smile his face into more lines than is in the new map with the
augmentation of the Indies.° You have not seen such a thing as
'tis: I can hardly forbear hurling things at him. I know my lady
will strike him. If she do, he'll smile, and take't for a great
favor.   70

SIR TOBY   Come bring us, bring us where he is.   *Exeunt.*

Scene iii   *Enter* SEBASTIAN *and* ANTONIO.

SEBASTIAN   I would not by my will have troubled you:
But since you make your pleasure of your pains,
I will no further chide you.

ANTONIO   I could not stay behind you. My desire
(More sharp than filèd steel) did spur me forth;   5
And not all° love to see you (though so much
As might have drawn one to a longer voyage),
But jealousy° what might befall your travel,
Being skilless in° these parts; which to a stranger,
Unguided and unfriended, often prove   10
Rough and unhospitable. My willing love,

(the last hatched was supposed to be the smallest)
fit of laughter

traitor to his faith (from Sp.)

incredible gaffes (or vul-
garaties)

56-71   Sir Toby forgets everything to greet Maria,
and she holds attention to the end of the scene when
she leads them both off in pursuit of Malvolio.
Most Marias enter laughing and speak only with
difficulty as if in "stitches" (58). Certainly her eager-
ness—images supplanting one another rapidly—
quickens tempo and expectation. Sir Toby's last
speech, in rhythm as in sense, helps the comic ball
to bounce forward.

teacher

(the first Mercator's map of
the world (1600) gave more
detail of the Americas and
East Indies)

<u>Scene iii</u>

1-19   For the third scene in succession the stage
is comparatively empty; but now only two people are
onstage throughout and the careful, parenthetical,
and qualifying phrases of Antonio's speech insist on
a slow and thoughtful tempo. The twinship of Viola
and Sebastian is not exploited here, for he is identified at once by Antonio's presence. Interest derives
chiefly from Antonio's conflicting desires to be with
Sebastian and, at the same time, to protect himself
from capture (see line 25). His uncertainty will be
shown physically as well as verbally, for he is on the
lookout in fear of capture and this effect is heightened by contrast with Sebastian's newfound assurance.
Sebastian uses the key word "will" from the

not only

anxiety
without knowledge of

The rather by° these arguments of fear,
Set forth in your pursuit.

SEBASTIAN   My kind Antonio,
  I can no other answer make but thanks,
  And thanks, and ever thanks; and oft good turns   15
  Are shuffled off with such uncurrent° pay.
  But were my worth,° as is my conscience, firm,
  You should find better dealing.° What's to do?
  Shall we go see the relics° of this town?

ANTONIO   Tomorrow sir; best first go see your lodging.   20

SEBASTIAN   I am not weary, and 'tis long to night.
  I pray you let us satisfy our eyes
  With the memorials and the things of fame
  That do renown this city.

ANTONIO   Would you'ld pardon me.
  I do not without danger walk these streets.   25
  Once in a sea-fight 'gainst the count his galleys,°
  I did some service; of such note indeed
  That were I ta'en here, it would scarce be answered.°

SEBASTIAN   Belike you slew great number of his people?

ANTONIO   Th' offense is not of such a bloody nature,   30
  Albeit the quality° of the time and quarrel
  Might well have given us bloody argument.°
  It might have since been answered in repaying
  What we took from them, which for traffic's° sake
  Most of our city did. Only myself stood out;   35
  For which, if I be lapsèd° in this place,
  I shall pay dear.

SEBASTIAN   Do not then walk too open.

ANTONIO   It doth not fit me. Hold sir, here's my purse.
  In the south suburbs at the Elephant°
  Is best to lodge. I will bespeak our diet,°   40
  Whiles you beguile the time, and feed your knowledge,
  With viewing of the town. There shall you have° me.

SEBASTIAN   Why I your purse?

increased by

play's subtitle in his first line: he is still fancy-free, whereas Antonio's "desire" and "love" make him live in danger as on a precipice. The repeated "thanks" (14-15) can suggest embarrassment, or may be played as if spoken in the face of Antonio's repeated but silent signs that there is no need for them.

i.e., useless
possessions, means
trading/behavior
historical sights

20-37 Antonio tries to hold Sebastian by mere business (see line 20). This has no effect and Antonio has to acknowledge—something he had tried to hide (see lines 9-11)—that the danger is particular to himself and, by implication, that he has risked his life for Sebastian.

the count's warships

compensated

circumstances
contention

trade's

caught without having made
compensation*

37-38 Sebastian's response to Antonio's danger is not to stay in hiding with him or to travel on to some other town but, rather, to give the easy and obvious advice that Antonio should be careful. "Hold sir" of the next line suggests that he had started to move off straight-away.

Having failed to restrain Sebastian, Antonio accepts this situation laconically. He then quickly offers his purse and turns to the business of accommodation: this will be a way of ensuring Sebastian's return, at least.

(an inn of this name was near
Globe Theatre)
order our meals

find

39-48 Sebastian makes no response to the gift of the purse or, perhaps, Antonio does not allow him opportunity to do so. When he does ask why he should be given money, the incomplete verse-line

ANTONIO   Haply your eye shall light upon some toy°
    You have desire to purchase, and your store°   45
    I think is not for idle markets,° sir.

SEBASTIAN   I'll be your purse-bearer, and leave you for
    An hour.

ANTONIO   To th' Elephant.

SEBASTIAN   I do remember.   *Exeunt.*

Scene iv   *Enter* OLIVIA *and* MARIA.

OLIVIA   I have sent after him.—He says he'll come.—
    How shall I feast him? What bestow of° him?
    For youth is bought more oft than begged or borrowed.°
    I speak too loud.—
    Where's Malvolio? He is sad and civil,°   5
    And suits well for a servant with my fortunes.
    Where is Malvolio?

MARIA   He's coming, madam; but in very strange manner. He
    is sure possessed,° madam.

OLIVIA   Why what's the matter? Does he rave?   10

MARIA   No madam, he does nothing but smile. Your ladyship
    were best to have some guard about you if he come, for sure
    the man is tainted in's wits.

OLIVIA   Go call him hither.

                        Enter MALVOLIO.

                        I am as mad as he,
    If sad and merry madness equal be.   15
    How now, Malvolio?

MALVOLIO   Sweet lady, ho, ho!

OLIVIA   Smil'st thou? I sent for thee upon a sad° occasion.

trifle
resources
casual purchases

suggests a pause before Antonio answers lightly, concealing the deeper motivation made explicit earlier. The climax to this scene is, therefore, muted, but alive with contrasts: Sebastian walks off freely; Antonio is apprehensive, only able to repeat an instruction.

Scene iv

1-14   Olivia enters ahead of Maria and is quick and nervous. The first verse-line of her speech breaks its phrasing and rhythm, and changes tense, after the sixth syllable, as her mind leaps forward to the imaginary reality of Cesario coming to her house, despite his vow not to do so (see III.i. 155-56). After line 3, she stops herself, looks around, sees Maria, recalls Malvolio, speaks to Maria, and pretends (once more) that she is sad and not hectically excited. With love, hope, danger, and fear her eyes are

on
young people are more often
    won by gifts than by plead-
    ing or promises
grave and respectful

alight and, in style, her speech is here as light as air. To Maria's careful description of Malvolio's madness, Olivia answers simply, since nothing could be more surprising than herself.

i.e., with a devil

14-15   This is Malvolio's most effective entry. At first he is silent, but he has much to do: he must have a "sad face" and "reverent carriage"; he must smile; he must overcome the discomfort of cross-gartering (see lines 19-20); and, while obeying all these contradictory commands, he must bring his dream of being "Count Malvolio" to the test of reality. Alternatively, however, he may do nothing extreme here, the actor using his first silence to show that Malvolio is almost petrified, is inwardly very afraid of what he had thought he wanted ("willed") above all other things.

Most editors move the entry to after line 15, but its position in the Folio, retained here, is dramatically effective. Maria turns to seek Malvolio and he—precisely then—enters saying nothing; soon he is silently smiling as boldly as he can. Olivia sees him but, as no one else speaks, turns aside for soliloquy. In this confrontation all three are helpless: Maria with suppressed laughter and delight, Malvolio with effort, and Olivia with the recognition that "I am as mad as he."

16-26   Olivia's concerned question (line 16) compels reply as all eyes, onstage and in the auditorium, are on Malvolio. What he says in reply is trite, vulgar,

serious

and, possibly, tongue-tied, making this encounter a

MALVOLIO   Sad, lady? I could be sad: this does make some obstruction in the blood, this cross-gartering; but what of that?   20
If it please the eye of one, it is with me as the very true son-
net° is, "Please one, and please all."°

OLIVIA   Why how dost thou, man? What is the matter with thee?

MALVOLIO   Not black in my mind, though yellow in my legs.° It
did come to his hands, and commands shall be executed. I   25
think we do know the sweet Roman hand.°

OLIVIA   Wilt thou go to bed, Malvolio?

MALVOLIO   To bed? Ay sweetheart, and I'll come to thee.

OLIVIA   God comfort thee. Why dost thou smile so, and kiss thy
hand so off?   30

MARIA   How do you, Malvolio?

MALVOLIO   At your request? Yes, nightingles answer daws!°

MARIA   Why appear you with this ridiculous boldness before my
lady?

MALVOLIO   "Be not afraid of greatness!" 'Twas well writ.   35

OLIVIA   What mean'st thou by that, Malvolio?

MALVOLIO   "Some are born great . . ."

OLIVIA   Ha?

MALVOLIO   "Some achieve greatness . . ."

OLIVIA   What say'st thou?   40

MALVOLIO   "And some have greatness thrust upon them."

OLIVIA   Heaven restore thee!

MALVOLIO   "Remember who commended thy yellow stockings . . ."

OLIVIA   Thy yellow stockings?   45

MALVOLIO   "And wished to see thee cross-gartered . . ."

OLIVIA   Cross-gartered?

MALVOLIO   "Go to, thou art made, if thou desir'st to be so . . ."

short poem   i.e., if I please
the one I love, the rest do
not matter

I am not melancholy in mind,
though my stockings are the
color of jealousy

italic handwriting (more fash-
ionable than the usual *secre-
tary* hand)

moment for comedy or for sympathy. Some Malvolios trip over their own feet, others tremble or stutter, others ogle and giggle, or look as if carried away in happiness; they all must smile. Laurence Olivier had entered and at once hid behind a large yew hedge teasing his lady; answering her, he peeped out of hiding, smiled broadly and waved his fingers vigorously; then he disappeared again, as suddenly as he had appeared. Should any sympathy be raised for the abused man, it will be quenched as soon as Malvolio proceeds to speak of his own discomfort and is entirely unmindful of Olivia's "sad occasion" (18). At line 22, he quotes a popular ballad to convey his self-satisfaction; some Malvolios sing it.

jackdaws (noisy, stupid birds)

27-34   Having failed to make any sense of what Malvolio is doing, Olivia thinks he must be seriously ill and therefore suggests he go to bed. He takes this as an invitation to lie with her and responds enthusiastically (see line 28), but nevertheless he still remains at a distance, smiling and kissing hands. His fantasy did not include intimacy and so, in obsessed self-satisfaction, he remains isolated, overweening, and impotent. He may show, or stumble over, his cross-gartered legs. At line 31, Maria probably has to go to him to ensure he hears a simple question.

35-51   Maria's insistence causes Malvolio to recite the grounds of his new confidence. Neither Olivia's questions, prayer, nor incredulous exclamations can stem the flow as Malvolio shows what love means to him and how he depends on the evidence of the letter. The actor must mark a growing ecstasy, pausing (as in the letter scene; see II.v) to "jet" and crow (and not, as might appear in a reading of the text, to allow Olivia to comment). A masturbatory excitement underlies his ecstatic speech.

In performance, all this is likely to be very funny, but a very intense Malvolio, his mind totally blinkered, could create a terrifying effect here that would stop all laughter.

OLIVIA   Am I made?°

MALVOLIO   "If not, let me see thee a servant still."   50

OLIVIA   Why this is very midsummer madness.°

Enter SERVANT.

SERVANT   Madam, the young gentleman of the Count Orsino's is
returned; I could hardly entreat him back. He attends your
ladyship's pleasure.

OLIVIA   I'll come to him. [*Exit* SERVANT.] Good Maria, let this   55
fellow be looked to. Where's my cousin Toby? Let some of
my people have a special care of him; I would not have him
miscarry° for the half of my dowry.

Exit [OLIVIA *with* MARIA.]

MALVOLIO   O ho, do you come near° me now? No worse man than
Sir Toby to look to me. This concurs directly with the letter: 60
she sends him on purpose that I may appear stubborn° to him,
for she incites me to that in the letter. "Cast thy humble slough,"
says she; "be opposite with a kinsman, surly with servants; let
thy tongue tang with arguments of state; put thyself into the
trick of singularity." And consequently sets down the manner   65
how: as a sad face, a reverend carriage, a slow tongue, in the
habit° of some sir° of note, and so forth. I have limed° her. But
it is Jove's doing, and Jove make me thankful. And when she
went away now, "Let this fellow° be looked to." "Fellow!" Not
"Malvolio," nor after my degree,° but "Fellow."—Why   70
everything adheres together, that no dram° of a scruple,° no
scruple of a scruple, no obstacle, no incredulous° or unsafe°
circumstance—what can be said? Nothing that can be,
can come between me and the full prospect of my hopes.
Well Jove, not I, is the doer of this, and he is to be thanked.   75

Enter SIR TOBY, FABIAN, *and* MARIA.

SIR TOBY   Which way is he, in the name of sanctity? If all the
devils of hell be drawn in little,° and Legion° himself possessed him, yet I'll speak to him.

(perhaps implying *mad,* or
maid)

extreme folly and license

52-58   Business and tone change suddenly with the servant's entry, the stage picture dissolving just as Malvolio reaches his climax: "What you will" is shown to be a precarious reality.

come to harm

i.e., begin to speak appropriately (and openly) about

stiff, harsh

clothing   gentleman
caught (as bird with birdlime)

servant (Malovio inteprets this as companion)

according to my position

small quantity   doubt/ $1/3$ dram

incredible   unreliable*

59-75   Malvolio might be expected to admit failure and so the actor may hesitate and speak slowly to play on that expectation. But as Malvolio cites the vital letter again, his speech gains momentum and rhythms again become more lively. The climax to his soliloquy is short—"I have limed her" (67)—and has no pretension to love or respect: Olivia is, for him, a snared bird; this is what he has "willed" and he thanks Jove for it.

The thought that Olivia has gone away, which earlier might have shattered his composure, has little effect now; even her dismissive "fellow" pleases him. He can also acknowledge his own earlier fears of what was "incredulous" and "unsafe" (72-73). Several times, syntax breaks down as his pleasure and confidence grow. Now Jove is introduced with "Well," not "But," and he no longer prays to be made "thankful." Laurence Olivier spoke the final "fellow" very softly and lingeringly, in luxurious self-indulgence. Malvolio has entered a silent daydream; he is yet more self-satisfied than before and oblivious of anything else.

assembed in small space
troop of evil spirits (biblical,
see *Mark* v.9)

76-106   At first, Malvolio adopts silence as the best response to Sir Toby and his companions, but then becomes "opposite" and "surly" as requested in the letter (see line 63). However, Maria's repetition of Olivia's words does catch his attention and so he is

FABIAN   Here he is, here he is!—How is't with you, sir?

SIR TOBY   How is't with you, man?   80

MALVOLIO   Go off; I discard you. Let me enjoy my private.° Go
off.

MARIA   Lo, how hollow the fiend speaks within him! Did not I
tell you?—Sir Toby, my lady prays you to have a care of him.

MALVOLIO   Aha, does she so?   85

SIR TOBY   Go to, go to; peace, peace; we must deal gently with
him. Let me alone.—How do you, Malvolio? How is't with
you? What, man, defy the devil! Consider, he's an enemy to
mankind.

MALVOLIO   Do you know what you say?   90

MARIA   La you, and you speak ill of the devil, how he takes it
at heart. Pray God he be not bewitched.

FABIAN   Carry his water° to th' wise° woman.

MARIA   Marry, and it shall be done tomorrow morning if I live.
My lady would not lose him for more than I'll say.   95

MALVOLIO   How now, mistress?

MARIA   O Lord.

SIR TOBY   Prithee hold thy peace; this is not the way. Do you not
see you move° him? Let me alone with him.

FABIAN   No way but gentleness: gently, gently. The fiend is   100
rough,° and will not be roughly used.

SIR TOBY   Why how now, my bawcock?° How dost thou chuck?°

MALVOLIO   Sir.

SIR TOBY   Ay, biddy,° come with me. What, man, 'tis not for
gravity to play at cherry-pit° with Satan. Hang him, foul   105
collier!°

MARIA   Get him to say his prayers, good Sir Toby, get him to
pray.

MALVOLIO   My prayers, minx?

privacy*

tricked into acknowledging his visitors. Their response is to pretend to be still more worried about his possession by a devil. With much comic show of bravery, Sir Toby advances alone at line 87 to reason with him and exhort him to fight the devil; Fabian provides a contrasting, and funnily deadpan, practicality (93). When Maria again quotes Olivia, her "O Lord" (97) may indicate that she is overcome with laughter at his immediate response. Sir Toby now sidles up to Malvolio in mock endearment and concern, ostensibly to humor the devil but truly to taunt his victim.

urine   (i.e., skilled in cures)

enrage

violent

fine fellow (Fr. *beau coq*)
    chick

chick

a dignified man must not play
    pitch and toss (for your
    soul)

coalman (proverbially, a
    cheater)

107-12 A smile, not assumed but real, is sometimes seen on Malvolio's face after "element" (112); his dream and self-esteem are unshaken and, "hereafter", he plans the total rout of his enemies. Alternatively, his persecutors' mock piety and show

MARIA   No, I warrant you; he will not hear of godliness.   110

MALVOLIO   Go hang yourselves all! You are idle° shallow things:
I am not of your element. You shall know more hereafter.

Exit.

SIR TOBY   Is't possible?

FABIAN   If this were played upon a stage now, I could condemn
it as an improbable fiction.   115

SIR TOBY   His very genius° hath taken the infection of the device,°
man.

MARIA   Nay, pursue him now, lest the device take air° and taint.°

FABIAN   Why, we shall make him mad indeed.

MARIA   The house will be the quieter.   120

SIR TOBY   Come, we'll have him in a dark room and bound.°
My niece is already in the belief that he's mad. We may
carry it° thus for our pleasure, and his penance, till our very
pastime, tired out of breath, prompt us to have mercy on
him; at which time, we will bring the device to the bar° and   125
crown thee for a finder of madmen. But see, but see.

Enter SIR ANDREW.

FABIAN   More matter for a May morning.°

SIR ANDREW   Here's the challenge; read it. I warrant there's
vinegar and pepper in't.

FABIAN   Is't so saucy?°   130

SIR ANDREW   Ay, is't, I warrant him. Do but read.

SIR TOBY   Give me. [*Reads.*] "Youth, whatsoever thou art, thou
art but a scurvy fellow."

FABIAN   Good, and valiant.

SIR TOBY   [*Reads.*] "Wonder not, nor admire° not in thy mind   135
why I do call thee so, for I will show thee no reason for't."

FABIAN   A good note; that keeps you from the blow of the law.

worthless

of fear cause Malvolio to lose patience so that, wrapping himself in what dignity can, he moves off at a far less dignified pace. Those remaining on stage, helpless with laughter and incredulity, are unable to follow.

guiding spirit   trick

become generally known
    spoil (lose its infectiousness)

119-26   Fabian, the one most aware of the improbabilities of their game (see lines 114-15), now makes the further point that Malvolio's madness could well become very real. Maria tersely accepts the possibility while Sir Toby goes on with his "pastime," assuming that "mercy" will eventually be possible (123-24). These three speeches can provide a still, sober moment in the developing hilarity, a close and revealing focus on the minds of each character in turn.

(usual treatment of madness)

continue the trick

submit the trick to public
    judgment

more fun for May Day festivities

127-52   Sir Andrew's entry is on the cue of "finder of madmen" (126) and Fabian notes this coincidence. The actor playing Sir Andrew will take this as an invitation to provide an absurd flourish and new burst of energy. When Sir Toby starts to read the letter, however, Sir Andrew falls silent. The latter takes Fabian's praise to heart and, during the reading, displays various mute signs of valor and of that "policy" (see III.ii.26) that he is supposed to hate, but which now may promise safety (see line 146).

piquant/impertinent

be surprised

SIR TOBY   [*Reads.*] "Thou com'st to the Lady Olivia, and in my
sight she uses thee kindly. But thou liest in thy throat: that
is not the matter I challenge thee for."   140

FABIAN   Very brief, and to exceeding good sense—less.

SIR TOBY   [*Reads.*] "I will waylay thee going home, where if it
be thy chance to kill me—"

FABIAN   Good.

SIR TOBY   [*Reads.*] "Thou kill'st me like a rogue and a villain."   145

FABIAN   Still you keep o' th' windy side° of the law. Good.

SIR TOBY   [*Reads.*] "Fare thee well, and God have mercy upon
one of our souls. He may have mercy upon mine, but my
hope is better, and so look to thyself. Thy friend as thou
usest him, and thy sworn enemy, ANDREW AGUECHEEK." 150
If this letter move him not, his legs cannot. I'll give't him.

MARIA   You may have very fit occasion for't. He is now in
some commerce° with my lady, and will by and by depart.

SIR TOBY   Go, Sir Andrew; scout me for him at the corner of the
orchard like a bum-baily.° So soon as ever thou seest him,   155
draw; and as thou draw'st, swear horrible; for it comes to
pass oft that a terrible oath, with a swaggering accent sharply
twanged off, gives manhood more approbation° than ever
proof° itself would have earned him. Away!

SIR ANDREW   Nay, let me alone for swearing.°   *Exit.*   160

SIR TOBY   Now will not I deliver his letter; for the behavior of
the young gentleman gives him out to be of good capacity°
and breeding; his employment between his lord and my niece
confirms no less. Therefore this letter, being so excellently
ignorant, will breed no terror in the youth; he will find it   165
comes from a clodpoll.° But sir, I will deliver his challenge
by word of mouth, set upon° Aguecheek a notable report° of
valor, and drive the gentleman (as I know his youth will
aptly° receive it) into a most hideous opinion of his rage,
skill, fury, and impetuosity. This will so fright them both   170
that they will kill one another by the look, like cockatrices.°

windward, safe side

147-48 Sir Toby often crosses himself on the prayer; Sir Andrew, following his lead, would then cross himself wildly, many times, so that he finishes up in comic confusion between true panic and false bravery.

talk

sheriff's officer (who made arrests for debts)

152-60 When Maria alerts them about Cesario's presence, Sir Andrew is sent into action. He will look abashed now that his moment has come, but recovers when Sir Toby reassures him by saying how effective swearing can be by itself, without fighting. The short line on his exit calls for an elaborate, climactic physical feat or absurdity if it is to have sufficient weight after nearly thirty lines of silence: Andrew will leave, confident once more, perhaps swearing loudly at random or brandishing his sword ridiculously.

confirmation
putting to a test

leave swearing to me

ability

161-71 As after Malvolio's exit, Shakespeare takes time to forward the plot. Sir Toby's speech commands silent attention until its completion with his ludicrous image of two frightened fighters; so Olivia enters to a renewed burst of laughter.

blockhead

give to   reputation for

readily

basilisks, fabulous reptiles able
to kill with a look

Enter OLIVIA *and* VIOLA.

FABIAN   Here he comes with your niece. Give them way° till he
take leave, and presently° after him.

SIR TOBY   I will meditate the while upon some horrid message
for a challenge.   [*Exeunt* SIR TOBY, FABIAN *and* MARIA.]   175

OLIVIA   I have said too much unto a heart of stone,
And laid° mine honor too unchary° out.
There's something in me that reproves my fault;
But such a headstrong potent fault it is
That it but mocks reproof.   180

VIOLA   With the same havior° that your passion bears
Goes on my master's grief.

OLIVIA   Here, wear this jewel° for me; 'tis my picture.
Refuse it not; it hath no tongue to vex you.
And I beseech you come again tomorrow.   185
What shall you ask of me that I'll deny,
That honor, saved,° may upon asking give?

VIOLA   Nothing but this: your true love for my master.

OLIVIA   How with mine honor may I give him that
Which I have given to you?

VIOLA   I will acquit you.   190

OLIVIA   Well, come again tomorrow. Fare thee well.
A fiend like thee° might bear my soul to hell.   [*Exit.*]

Enter SIR TOBY *and* FABIAN

SIR TOBY   Gentleman, God save thee.

VIOLA   And you, sir.   194

SIR TOBY   That defense thou hast, betake thee to't. Of what nature
the wrongs are thou hast done him, I know not; but thy
intercepter, full of despite,° bloody as the hunter, attends°
thee at the orchard end. Dismount° thy tuck,° be yare° in thy
preparation, for thy assailant is quick, skillful, and deadly.   199

VIOLA   You mistake sir; I am sure no man hath any quarrel to me.

let them do what they wish
instantly

172-75   The plotters quickly and conspiratorially disappear, perhaps into the same box tree as in the letter scene (ll.v).

displayed / risked   openly /
   carelessly

behavior

ornament, locket (?)

kept safe

176-92   At first, Olivia's speech has longer, steadier rhythms than when she last spoke and she can now acknowledge her "headstrong" feelings with composure. The incomplete line 180 indicates a pause after which Viola responds to Olivia's predicament, choosing her words to sound firm and reasoned. A second pause is indicated before Olivia replies, and then her composure is gone: rhythms are again short and urgent; she allows no time for her gift to be refused but "beseeches" Cesario to return.

When Viola replies shortly and firmly, Olivia quickly bids farewell and, in a last line (192), expresses her fear, guilt, excitement, and longing with complete and contrasting frankness. Olivia's ability to control herself has been precarious; she probably runs from the stage, leaving Viola speechless.

in your likeness

193-217   Sir Toby, bent on alarming Cesario, will speak fiercely; so Viola's first reply may be startled and followed immediately with an attempt to leave the stage—to be recalled by Sir Toby. After line 202, Viola may assume that she has cleared herself and smile winningly; but Sir Toby is unmoved and her smile and confidence will soon die. Sir Toby continues with forceful rhythms, piling epithets on each other to develop Cesario's fears to nightmare proportions. His citation of three deaths is often spoken slowly, so that it provides an unavoidable picture of horror for Viola. She is now ready to return to Olivia

defiance   awaits
draw (usually used of guns
   cannon)   rapier
   prompt

My remembrance is very free and clear from any image of
offense done to any man.

SIR TOBY   You'll find it otherwise, I assure you. Therefore, if you
hold your life at any price, betake you to your guard; for
your opposite hath in him what youth, strength, skill, and   205
wrath can furnish man withal.

VIOLA   I pray you sir, what is he?

SIR TOBY   He is knight, dubbed with unhatched° rapier and on
carpet consideration,° but he is a devil in private brawl.
Souls and bodies hath he divorced three; and his incense-   210
ment at this moment is so implacable that satisfaction can be
none, but by pangs of death and sepulcher. "Hob, nob"° is
his word; "give't or take't."

VIOLA   I will return again into the house, and desire some con-
duct° of the lady. I am no fighter. I have heard of some kind   215
of men that put quarrels purposely on others, to taste° their
valor: belike this is a man of that quirk.

SIR TOBY   Sir, no. His indignation derives itself out of a very
competent° injury; therefore get you on, and give him his   219
desire. Back you shall not to the house, unless you undertake
that with me, which with as much safety you might answer
him. Therefore on, or strip your sword stark naked; for meddle°
you must, that's certain, or forswear to wear iron about you.

VIOLA   This is as uncivil as strange. I beseech you do me this
courteous office, as to know of the knight what my offense   225
to him is. It is something of my negligence, nothing of my
purpose.

SIR TOBY   I will do so. Signior Fabian, stay you by this gentleman
till my return.   *Exit.*

VIOLA   Pray you sir, do you know of this matter?   230

FABIAN   I know the knight is incensed against you, even to a
mortal arbitrament;° but nothing of the circumstance more.

VIOLA   I beseech you, what manner of man is he?

FABIAN   Nothing of that wonderful promise, to read him by his   234
form, as you are like to find him in the proof of his valor. He is,

(from whom she has just escaped) and her male disguise drops completely with "I am no fighter." Her discomfiture is greater in that she had been feeling more at ease in her male disguise, being able deal firmly with Olivia: she should show the alarm of an impostor revealed, or an actor left without words or costume.

unused, unhacked (?)*
through court favor

have, or have not

escort
test

sufficient

engage in fight

218-33   At Hartford Stage in 1985, Viola "fairly quivers with trepidation, picking up her sword by the tip and rushing into retreat" (*New York Times*, 11 October, 1985). Sir Toby's words (and probably actions) prevent Viola's escape three or four times; he also threatens to fight her himself (and has perhaps drawn his sword). Now Viola begins to regain a male style of speech and, presumably, of action; but her pertness and confidence are gone. Left alone with Fabian, she first prays and then beseeches for help.

decision by a fight to the death

indeed sir, the most skillful, bloody, and fatal opposite that
you could possibly have found in any part of Illyria. Will you
walk towards him? I will make your peace with him, if I can.

VIOLA   I shall be much bound to you for't: I am one that had   239
rather go with sir priest than sir knight. I care not who knows
so much of my mettle.°   *Exeunt.*

Enter SIR TOBY *and* SIR ANDREW.

SIR TOBY   Why man, he's a very devil; I have not seen such a
firago.° I had a pass° with him, rapier, scabbard, and all; and
he gives me the stuck-in° with such a mortal motion° that it is
inevitable; and on the answer,° he pays you as surely as your   245
feet hits the ground they step on.° They say he has been fencer
to the Sophy.°

SIR ANDREW   Pox on't, I'll not meddle with him.

SIR TOBY   Ay, but he will not now be pacified: Fabian can scarce
hold him yonder.   250

SIR ANDREW   Plague on't, and I thought he had been valiant, and
so cunning in fence,° I'd have seen him damned ere I'd
have challenged him. Let him let the matter slip, and I'll give
him my horse, gray Capilet.

SIR TOBY   I'll make the motion.° Stand here; make a good show   255
on't. This shall end without the perdition of souls.° [*Aside.*]
Marry, I'll ride your horse as well as I ride you.

Enter FABIAN *and* VIOLA.

[*Aside to* FABIAN.] I have his horse to take up° the quarrel. I
have persuaded him the youth's a devil.

FABIAN   [*Aside.*] He is as horribly conceited of him;° and pants,   260
and looks pale, as if a bear were at his heels.

SIR TOBY   [*To* VIOLA.] There's no remedy sir: he will fight with
you for's oath sake. Marry, he hath better bethought him of
his quarrel, and he finds that now scarce to be worth talking
of. Therefore draw for the supportance° of his vow; he pro-   265
tests he will not hurt you.

courage/sword

239-41 Encouraged by Fabian's talk of "peace" (see line 238), Viola here attempts a joke; perhaps she tries to laugh off the matter with what she thinks of as male brashness.

virago (pun on *fire* ?)   bout
stoccado, thrust   deadly
   drive
return
as certain as you are laid flat
Shah of Persia

241 The quick exits and re-entries broaden the humor and give a sense of impending comic chaos. Sir Toby is probably pulling or pushing the fearful Sir Andrew onto the stage, unaware that Viola has bolted.

at fencing

249-50 Fabian will be heard, and perhaps seen, struggling with Viola in an attempt to bring her back to the fight. (The "peace" talks have already broken down.) Probably Sir Toby is also holding Sir Andrew, by force, from escape.

offer

i.e. loss of life

255-56 Making "a good show", Sir Andrew would strike a (ludicrous) warlike attitude but the reference to "perdition of souls" is often taken as a hint for Sir Andrew to panic and fall on his knees in prayer.

resolve

has the same terrifying notion
   of Sir Andrew

258-66 Somehow, in the gathering confusion, Sir Toby and Fabian exchange notes, while keeping their eyes (at least) on the reluctant combatants and doing their comic best to prevent them from seeing each other. They either hold their victims at arm's length or set them to prepare for the duel with such frightening and frenzied zeal that neither of them can move or speak; both may be on their knees, or one or both may have climbed up into a very large box tree. During the asides, there are three centers of interest and farcical opportunities in plenty.

carrying out

VIOLA   [*Aside.*] Pray God defend me! A little thing would
        make me tell them how much I lack of a man.

FABIAN   Give ground if you see him furious.

SIR TOBY   Come Sir Andrew, there's no remedy; the gentleman   270
        will for his honor's sake have one bout with you; he cannot by
        the duello° avoid it; but he has promised me, as he is a gentle-
        man and a soldier, he will not hurt you. Come on, to't.

SIR ANDREW   Pray God he keep his oath!   [*Draws.*]

                    Enter ANTONIO.

VIOLA   I do assure you 'tis against my will.   [*Draws.*]   275

ANTONIO   [*Draws.*] Put up your sword. If this young gentleman
        Have done offense, I take the fault on me;
        If you offend him, I for him defy you.

SIR TOBY   You, sir? Why, who are you?

ANTONIO   One sir, that for his love dares yet do more   280
        Than you have heard him brag to you he will.

SIR TOBY   Nay, if you be an undertaker,° I am for you. [*Draws.*]

                    Enter OFFICERS.

FABIAN   O good Sir Toby, hold! Here come the officers.

SIR TOBY   [*To* ANTONIO.] I'll be with you anon.   284

VIOLA   [*To* SIR ANDREW.] Pray sir, put your sword up, if you please.

SIR ANDREW   Marry, will I, sir; and for that° I promised you, I'll be
        as good as my word. He will bear you easily, and reins well.

FIRST OFFICER   This is the man; do thy office.°

SECOND OFFICER   Antonio, I arrest thee at the suit
        Of Count Orsino.

ANTONIO   You do mistake me, sir.   290

FIRST OFFICER   No sir, no jot. I know your favor° well,
        Though now you have no sea-cap on your head.

267-68   Viola's aside can be a moment of true and earnest prayer or a further step in either comic panic or ironic self-judgment.

code of honor governing duels

274-78   The timing of Antonio's entrance suggests that Viola and Sir Andrew do no more fighting than face each other. (Some Violas whisper or shout line 275 to Sir Andrew.) But in many productions, Antonio's immediately strong and effective entry is delayed so that an absurdly reluctant combat is allowed to develop and the comedy reach a speechless climax of absurdity.

one who takes up a challenge,*
   helper

283-93   Fabian and Sir Toby probably hide once more where they had done on Olivia's entry at line 172. As soon as Antonio draws his sword (see line 276), Viola and Sir Andrew may run into each other's arms in sheer panic at the new intrusion, so that they can now whisper together, relieved to have escaped

as for what (i.e., his horse)
yet another danger.

   The formal speech of the officers changes rhythm, tone, and dramatic focus in a moment.

duty

face

Take him away; he knows I know him well.

ANTONIO   I must obey. [*To* VIOLA.] This comes with seeking you.
But there's no remedy; I shall answer it.   295
What will you do, now my necessity
Makes me to ask you for my purse? It grieves me
Much more for what I cannot do for you
Than what befalls myself. You stand amazed,
But be of comfort.   300

SECOND OFFICER   Come sir, away.

ANTONIO   I must entreat of you some of that money.

VIOLA   What money, sir?
For the fair kindness you have showed me here,
And part° being prompted by your present trouble,   305
Out of my lean and low ability°
I'll lend you something. My having is not much.
I'll make division of my present° with you.
Hold, there's half my coffer.°

ANTONIO   Will you deny me now?
Is't possible that my deserts to you   310
Can lack persuasion?° Do not tempt my misery,
Lest that it make me so unsound° a man
As to upbraid you with those kindnesses
That I have done for you.

VIOLA   I know of none,
Nor know I you by voice, or any feature.   315
I hate ingratitude more in a man
Than lying, vainness,° babbling,° drunkenness,
Or any taint of vice whose strong corruption
Inhabits our frail blood.

ANTONIO   O heavens themselves!

SECOND OFFICER   Come sir, I pray you go.   320

ANTONIO   Let me speak a little. This youth that you see here,
I snatched one half out of the jaws of death,
Relieved him with such sanctity of love;
And to his image, which methought did promise
Most venerable worth, did I devotion.°   325

294-303 Antonio is more sorrowful at parting from Sebastian than concerned for his own safety; his words surprise and perplex not only Viola, but all his hearers.

300-06 Incomplete verse-lines (300, 301, 303) indicate pauses in which Viola does not, and cannot, respond to Antonio's varied appeals.

partly
funds

304-11 Viola's neat and nimble words show returning confidence (see also lines 314-19). She forgets herself by thinking what to do when she sees someone else in need; but her very promptness will exacerbate Antonio's sense of outrage.

what I have now
moneybox

power to persuade
lacking in judgment

312-35 At line 319, Antonio is almost speechless, but controls himself in order to attempt rational discourse. That failing, he tries again to make Cesario, whom he takes for Sebastian, understand his feelings. By line 317, he is again exclaiming with short, loaded sentences and, at this point, he seems to become "mad" (333), as Olivia and Malvolio have done before; also like them, he shows his "passion" (336). Only now does he use the name "Sebastian", offering a clue about what is happening to Viola but at a time when he can no longer listen to what she might say.

boastfulness   prating

idolized him as one who
   seemed sure to prove wor-
   thy of esteem

FIRST OFFICER   What's that to us? The time goes by. Away.

ANTONIO   But, O how vile an idol proves this god!
Thou hast, Sebastian, done good feature shame.
In nature, there's no blemish but the mind;°
None can be called deformed but the unkind.°   330
Virtue is beauty; but the beautous evil
Are empty trunks° o'erflourished° by the devil.

FIRST OFFICER   The man grows mad; away with him! Come,
come sir.

ANTONIO   Lead me on.   *Exit [with* OFFICERS.]   335

VIOLA   Methinks his words do from such passion fly
That he believes himself; so do not I.
Prove true, imagination, O prove true,
That I, dear brother, be now ta'en for you!

SIR TOBY   Come hither, knight; come hither, Fabian. We'll whis- 340
per o'er a couplet or two of most sage saws.°

VIOLA   He named Sebastian. I my brother know
Yet living in my glass.° Even such and so
In favor was my brother, and he went
Still in this fashion, color, ornament,   345
For him I imitate. O if it prove,
Tempests are kind, and salt waves fresh in love!   [*Exit.*]

SIR TOBY   A very dishonest° paltry boy, and more a coward than
a hare. His dishonesty appears in leaving his friend here in necessity, and denying him; and for his cowardship, ask Fabian.

FABIAN   A coward, a most devout coward; religious in it.°   351

SIR ANDREW   'Slid,° I'll after him again, and beat him.

SIR TOBY   Do; cuff him soundly, but never draw thy sword.

SIR ANDREW   And I do not . . .   [*Exit.*]

FABIAN   Come, let's see the event.°   355

SIR TOBY   I dare lay any money, 'twill be nothing yet.°

                                        Exit [with FABIAN.]

(as opposed to outward appearance, or *feature*)

ungrateful, unnatural

chests   decorated*

335   Antonio believes he is in danger of death (see III.iii.28, 37) but his new brevity suggests he is now without further hope: since Sebastian has proved false, he allows himself to be taken offstage without further resistance. He does not see Viola's dawning joy, soon to be expressed with springing rhythm, couplets, and ringing tones.

340-41   Sir Toby re-emerges with conspiratorial words and actions so that he too fails to see the change in Cesario.

wise sayings

i.e., looking at me from my mirror

347   Viola is ready to believe her imagination rather than her fears—in this, facing a somewhat similar situation to that which had made Malvolio look such a fool. She is transformed from a pathetic-comic coward to a generous and affectionate sister: this provides the climax for the long scene, Sir Toby being out of earshot and other events at a standstill.

dishonorable

dedicated to it

by God's eyelid

354-56   Sir Andrew goes offstage in mid-sentence, like a shot from a gun; probably he has already started to beat the air in the absence of his intended victim (see line 352). Sir Toby will leave more slowly than Fabian who has to rally him. Accompanying a delayed exit, a melancholy or discouraged speaking of line 356 can draw an audience's attention to deep cynicism underlying Sir Toby's almost constant geniality.

outcome

after all

ACT IV

Scene i   *Enter* SEBASTIAN *and* CLOWN.

CLOWN   Will you make me believe that I am not sent for you?

SEBASTIAN   Go to, go to, thou art a foolish fellow. Let me be
clear of thee.

CLOWN   Well held out,° i' faith! No, I do not know you; nor I
am not sent to you by my lady, to bid you come speak with   5
her; nor your name is not Master Cesario; nor this is not
my nose° neither. Nothing that is so, is so.

SEBASTIAN   I prithee vent° thy folly somewhere else,—thou
know'st not me.

CLOWN   Vent my folly! He has heard that word of some great   10
man, and now applies it to a fool. Vent my folly! I am afraid
this great lubber,° the world, will prove a cockney.° I prithee
now, ungird° thy strangeness,° and tell me what I shall vent
to my lady. Shall I vent to her that thou art coming?

SEBASTIAN   I prithee, foolish Greek,° depart from me. There's   15
money for thee; if you tarry longer, I shall give worse
payment.

CLOWN   By my troth, thou hast an open hand.° These wise men
that give fools money, get themselves a good report, after
fourteen years' purchase.°   20

Enter SIR ANDREW, SIR TOBY, *and* FABIAN.

SIR ANDREW   Now sir, have I met you again? There's for you!
                                         [*Strikes* SEBASTIAN.]

SEBASTIAN   Why there's for thee, and there, and there!

ACT IV. Scene i

1　　　Feste, who elsewhere plays successfully with everyone else's sense of what *is*, here meets absolute disbelief; he has to pursue Sebastian, who is trying to escape. So starts a short scene which is alive with incomprehension and violent exertion: Sebastian believing everyone is "mad" (see line 23), while they all believe that they are dealing with Cesario. As Sir Toby draws his sword (see lines 37-38), the comedy is on the point of becoming a fight in earnest. Antonio had told Sebastian that Illyria was dangerous, so he will not hold back.

maintained

(pun on *no*; or with phallic gesture)

discharge, express

　　　　Shakespeare has used the twinship of Viola and Sebastian to give maximum dramatic excitement before the comedy draws to its close. In Elizabethan performances where boys played girls, the audience may be momentarily mistaken too; this is the first time Sebastian has entered without Antonio to identify him.

lout　　　weakling, fop

unbelt　　　aloofness/oddity

(var. of *merry Greek* = one of the boys, rowdy)

15-24　　　Calling Feste a fool for the third time, Sebastian dismisses him with payment (as Orsino and Viola have already done). Feste still believes Cesario has fooled him and mockingly calls him a "wise" man.

art generous

　　　　Sebastian turns from one fool, only to run straight into another in the person of Sir Andrew. Absurdity increases rapidly as Sebastian repays one blow with three, Sir Andrew falls silent in surprise, incomprehension, and fright, and Sir Toby and Fabian put an armlock on Sebastian from the rear or in some other way manhandle him.

i.e., it will be long before it is paid for

　　　　Line 23, if spoken in confidence to the audience, can be broadly comic; if spoken in perplexity, while looking at all the players onstage, it can comment on the whole play, the *Twelfth Night* disguises and license.

[*Strikes* Sir Andrew.]
Are all the people mad?

Sir Toby   Hold sir, or I'll throw your dagger o'er the house.

[*Seizes* Sebastian.]

Clown   This will I tell my lady straight.° I would not be in some   25
of your coats for twopence.   [*Exit.*]

Sir Toby   Come on sir; hold.

Sir Andrew   Nay let him alone; I'll go another way to work
with him. I'll have an action of battery against him,° if
there be any law in Illyria. Though I struck him first, yet   30
it's no matter for that.

Sebastian   Let go thy hand.

Sir Toby   Come sir, I will not let you go. Come my young
soldier, put up your iron. You are well fleshed.° Come on.

Sebastian   I will be free from thee.   [*Frees himself, and draws.*]
What wouldst thou now?   35
If thou dar'st tempt me further, draw thy sword.

Sir Toby   What, what? Nay then, I must have an ounce or two
of this malapert° blood from you.   [*Draws.*]

Enter Olivia.

Olivia   Hold Toby! On thy life I charge thee hold!

Sir Toby   Madam.   40

Olivia   Will it be ever thus? Ungracious° wretch,
Fit for the mountains and the barbarous caves,
Where manners ne'er were preached! Out of my sight!—
Be not offended, dear Cesario.—
Rudesby,° begone.—
[*Exeunt* Sir Toby, Sir Andrew, *and* Fabian.]
I prithee gentle friend,   45
Let thy fair wisdom, not thy passion, sway°
In this uncivil and unjust extent°
Against thy peace. Go with me to my house,
And hear thou there how many fruitless pranks

immediately

charge him with assaulting me

emboldened by drawing blood

32-40   As two very capable men face each other with drawn swords, the scene becomes still and silent with danger. At this moment, Olivia enters and takes command, danger giving urgency to her speech so that Sir Toby is deflated to a one-word acceptance.

impudent

rude, reprobate

insolent lout

rule

barbarous and unlawful
   assault

41-53   Not long before this, Olivia, who had sought cloistered seclusion, confessed to her own "unmuzzled thoughts" (see III.i.112), but now she dismisses barbarity scornfully and, in almost the same breath, speaks to "dear Cesario" as to a "gentle friend" (44.45). Command of herself cannot be easy and Sebastian will be the more amazed at this mixture of authority and obvious emotion. When Olivia calls him Cesario, as the fool had done, and when she praises his "wisdom" (46), he fears that he is mad, as well as everyone else (55). "Nay come" (58) suggests that he has moved apart from Olivia, at first to collect his wits and then to ignore them.
   As Sebastian chooses "fancy" (56) before common sense (the word means both imagination

This ruffian hath botched up,° that thou thereby   50
Mayst smile at this: thou shalt not choose° but go;
Do not'deny. Beshrew° his soul for me;
He started° one poor heart° of mine, in thee.

SEBASTIAN   What relish is in this? How runs the stream?
Or° I am mad, or else this is a dream.   55
Let fancy still my sense° in Lethe° steep;
If it be thus to dream, still° let me sleep!

OLIVIA   Nay come, I prithee. Would thou'dst be ruled by me!

SEBASTIAN   Madam, I will.

OLIVIA   O say so, and so be!   *Exeunt.*

Scene ii   *Enter* MARIA *and* CLOWN.

MARIA   Nay, I prithee put on this gown, and this beard; make him
    believe thou art Sir Topas the curate;° do it quickly. I'll call Sir
    Toby the whilst.   [*Exit.*]

CLOWN   Well, I'll put it on, and I will dissemble° myself in't,
    and I would I were the first that ever dissembled° in such a   5
    gown. I am not tall enough to become the function well, nor
    lean enough to be thought a good student; but to be said an
    honest man and a good housekeeper goes as fairly as to say a
    careful° man and a great scholar. The competitors° enter.

                Enter SIR TOBY [*and* MARIA.]

SIR TOBY   Jove bless thee, Master Parson.   10

CLOWN   *Bonos dies,*° Sir Toby; for, as the old hermit of Prague,°
    that never saw pen and ink, very wittily said to a niece of
    King Gorboduc,° "That that is, is"; so I, being Master
    Parson, am Master Parson; for what is "that" but that? and
    "is" but is ?   15

SIR TOBY   To him, Sir Topas.

crudely attempted
have no alternative
confound
startled   (i.e., the heart she
   has given to Cesario; pun
   on *hart*)
either
reason   (river of oblivion
   in Hades)
always

and sexual desire) couplets have already begun to mark and propel this dialogue step by step forward. He is being led to accept a dream as reality and to speak of "what he wills" (see lines 57, 59); on "I will," Sebastian probably sheathes his sword. Olivia can now say little but "so be!", but some actresses speak her first "O" as a long and inarticulate expression of surprise and delight.

After the last word in the scene, the two must come together, as if in a dream, and leave in a shared silence. Sometimes they hold hands, as if trying to gain some sense of reality; usually they leave without ceasing to gaze into each other's eyes. The rapt, mutual response that is needed to take the two characters offstage is a great change from the conflicts and noise that preceded it only moments before, and also a notable piece of silent drama.

Scene ii

parish priest

disguise
played the hypocrite

careworn   confederates

good day   (invented personage)
(legendary British king; no *niece* is known)

1   The purpose of Maria's business is not clear until line 18, so interest centers at first on her haste and calling of Sir Toby, and then on Feste's priestly disguise. Anything might happen now, would think an audience unfamiliar with the text, especially after Sebastian and Olivia have just gone off stage together, suddenly able to enjoy their fancies and ready to be "ruled" by each other (IV.i.56-9).

4-9   After some reluctance (see 'Nay," line 1) and a soliloquy that allows him to address the audience in his own voice on the subject of dissembling, Feste notices the others enter and swiftly finishes disguising himself and takes up his pose as Sir Topas. As the fool is transformed into the careful scholar, the audience will know that a trap is being set, but its purpose has still not been stated.

10-11   Sir Toby joins in the make-believe with his pious greeting and so shows that Maria has told him about the trick; Feste answers in an assumed personical voice (see line 60).

13-15   A paradoxical reversal of "Nothing that is so, is so" (IV.i.7; i.e., "deceit can be found everywhere"): now that Feste is in disguise he anticipates the new situation in which whatever he does can be taken as real.

CLOWN   What ho, I say. Peace in° this prison!

SIR TOBY   The knave° counterfeits well; a good knave.

MALVOLIO *within.*

MALVOLIO   Who calls there?

CLOWN   Sir Topas the curate, who comes to visit Malvolio the   20
lunatic.

MALVOLIO   Sir Topas, Sir Topas, good Sir Topas, go to my lady.

CLOWN   Out,° hyperbolical° fiend! How vexest thou this man!
Talkest thou nothing but of ladies?

SIR TOBY   Well said, Master Parson.   25

MALVOLIO   Sir Topas, never was man thus wronged; good Sir
Topas, do not think I am mad. They have laid° me here in
hideous darkness.

CLOWN   Fie, thou dishonest° Satan. I call thee by the most mod-
est° terms, for I am one of those gentle ones that will use the   30
devil himself with courtesy. Say'st thou that house° is dark?

MALVOLIO   As hell, Sir Topas.

CLOWN   Why it hath bay windows transparent as barricadoes,°
and the clerestories° toward the south north are as lustrous
as ebony; and yet complainest thou of obstruction?°   35

MALVOLIO   I am not mad Sir Topas; I say to you this house is dark.

CLOWN   Madman thou errest: I say there is no darkness but igno-
rance° in which thou art more puzzled° than the Egyptians
in their fog.°

MALVOLIO   I say this house is as dark as ignorance, though igno-   40
rance were as dark as hell; and I say there was never man
thus abused. I am no more mad than you are; make the trial
of it in any constant question.°

CLOWN   What is the opinion of Pythagoras° concerning wild
fowl?   45

MALVOLIO   That the soul of our grandam might happily° inhabit a
bird.

(usual greeting of priest on
entering a home)

fellow

19 Malvolio's prison is often a trapdoor in the stage with a grill fixed beneath; this makes Malvolio's description of it as "hell" (32) particularly appropriate, for the space under the stage at the Globe Theatre was so named. Sometimes Malvolio is shown behind a door with a grill, or one with a chain so that it opens only a crack. The purpose of Feste's disguise is now clear.

Malvolio plays the whole scene with only his hands and blear-eyed face struggling to communicate from within his confinement. Some actors accentuate his pain: Michael Hordern played him at the Old Vic, London "as if he were indeed mad: his face is tortured; his hands, reaching out of the pit . . suggest the damned in the Inferno. The whole performance is too uncomfortable to be really amusing. One laughed, but one also shivered" (*Spectator*, 15 January 1954).

fie   extravagant, outrageous

Henry Irving, in 1884, broke with custom and was "seen actually visible, chained as a madman, and recumbent on his pallet: he rose to tragic dignity and passion. The yellow stockings, the cross-gartering, the amblings, the leerings, the hand-kissing of the steward, dreaming that he was to be 'the Count Malvolio,'...all disappear; and we are confronted by a Man, desperately wounded in his self-love, exasperated by insult and outrage, but determined to assert and to vindicate his manhood" (*Illustrated London News*, 12 July).

imprisoned, cast down

shameful, lewd

mildest

madman's cell

At the American Repertory Theatre, Cambridge, Mass. in 1989, the chief effect was "the Grand Guignold cruelty faced by Malvolio"(*New York Times*, 20 December).

barricades

upper windows

shutting out of light

23-35 Feste, like Sir Toby in III.iv, pretends that it is not Malvolio speaking but a fiend who has taken possession of him. Malvolio maintains a helpless silence, or perhaps emits a maddened laugh, before protesting against the charge of lunacy. As if speaking to Satan, Feste continues to reason with infuriating gentleness that what is not, is.

(biblical; see *Ephesians* iv. 18)
   bewildered

(a plague of *thick darkness*; biblical; see *Exodus* x.21-23)

32 Malvolio ceases to explain or ask for favors, but gives an anguished cry, or a comic, matter-of-fact acceptance of Feste's question to the fiend.

36-43 Malvolio twice stresses "I," asking to be accepted as he is: Feste does so, taking him as a madman. (This is the moment remembered by Feste later, to taunt Malvolio: see V.i.355-57.) Malvolio eagerly accepts the opportunity to argue reasonably, again stressing "I say...I say...I am."

formal examination

(Greek philosopher who theo-
   rized about transmigration
   of souls to animals)

perhaps

44-54 When he answers confidently and ex-

CLOWN   What think'st thou of his opinion?

MALVOLIO   I think nobly of the soul, and no way approve his
  opinion.   50

CLOWN   Fare thee well. Remain thou still in darkness: thou shalt
  hold th' opinion of Pythagoras, ere I will allow of thy wits,°
  and fear to kill a woodcock,° lest thou dispossess the soul of
  thy grandam. Fare thee well.

MALVOLIO   Sir Topas, Sir Topas!   55

SIR TOBY   My most exquisite° Sir Topas!

CLOWN   Nay, I am for all waters.°

MARIA   Thou mightst have done this without thy beard and gown;
  he sees thee not.

SIR TOBY   To him in thine own voice, and bring me word how   60
  thou find' st him. [*To* MARIA.] I would we were well rid of this
  knavery. If he may be conveniently delivered, I would he
  were; for I am now so far in offense with my niece that I cannot
  pursue with any safety this sport to the upshot.°—Come by and
  by to my chamber.   *Exit* [SIR TOBY *and* MARIA.]   65

CLOWN   [*Sings.*]   "Hey Robin, jolly Robin,°
                          Tell me how thy lady does."

MALVOLIO   Fool.

CLOWN   [*Sings.*]   "My lady is unkind, perdie."°

MALVOLIO   Fool.   70

CLOWN   [*Sings.*]   "Alas,' why is she so?"

MALVOLIO   Fool, I say.

CLOWN   [*Sings.*]   "She loves another."—Who calls, ha?

MALVOLIO   Good fool, as ever thou wilt deserve well at my hand,
  help me to a candle, and pen, ink, and paper. As I am a   75
  gentleman, I will live to be thankful to thee for't.

CLOWN   Master Malvolio?

MALVOLIO   Ay, good fool.

presses his own sense of human dignity, Malvolio is mocked by Feste at the very point where he thinks himself most secure. Feste's response implies the charge of over-confidence, of thinking fools ("woodcock") are no kin to himself.

admit your sanity
(proverbially, stupid bird)

55   With "Fare thee well" (54), Feste had left Malvolio's prison to talk to Sir Toby; sometimes its door or grill has been shut, so that Malvolio's cry is muffled as well as frustrated and infuriated, or, possibly, pathetic.

ingenious

can assume any quality

60-65   Maria was eager at the beginning of the scene to see the baiting of Malvolio and she says nothing here to Sir Toby's warning that the sport has been taken too far. Her silent exit at the same time as Sir Toby's is the last contribution she makes to the play, so that how she leaves is a matter of importance to the audience's view of her: does she leave with Sir Toby, or before or after him? Later the audience hears that Sir Toby has married her.

final shot (in archery)

(from an old ballad)

"Come by and by to my chamber" is usually spoken to Feste; but it can be addressed to Maria, as the invitation which will, off stage, lead to a proposal of marriage.

indeed

73-89   With the last line of his "jolly" (66) song, Feste tells Malvolio the truth about Olivia and leaves no time after this for Malvolio's refrain of "Fool." However, Malvolio does not get the message, because he is now intent on self-justification. At lines 80-81, he is tricked into likening himself to a fool but he gives no sign that he realizes what he has said. In case the grip on his own dignity should be slackening, Feste brings back Sir Topas to confuse him still more.

CLOWN   Alas sir, how fell you besides your five wits?°

MALVOLIO   Fool, there was never man so notoriously abused; I   80
am as well in my wits, fool as thou art.

CLOWN   But as well? Then you are mad indeed, if you be no
better in your wits than a fool.

MALVOLIO   They have here propertied me;° keep me in darkness,
send ministers to me, asses, and do all they can to face° me   85
out of my wits.

CLOWN   Advise you° what you say; the minister is here.—
Malvolio, Malvolio, thy wits the heavens restore. Endeavor
thyself to sleep, and leave thy vain bibble-babble.°

MALVOLIO   Sir Topas.   90

CLOWN   Maintain° no words with him, good fellow.—Who, I,
sir? Not I, sir. God buy° you, good Sir Topas.—Marry,
amen.—I will sir. I will.

MALVOLIO   Fool, fool, fool, I say!

CLOWN   Alas sir, be patient. What say you, sir? I am shent° for   95
speaking to you.

MALVOLIO   Good fool, help me to some light and some paper. I
tell thee, I am as well in my wits as any man in Illyria.

CLOWN   Well-a-day° that you were, sir.

MALVOLIO   By this hand, I am. Good fool, some ink, paper, and   100
light; and convey what I will set down to my lady. It shall
advantage thee more than ever the bearing of letter did.

CLOWN   I will help you to't. But tell me true, are you not mad indeed, or do you but counterfeit?

MALVOLIO   Believe me, I am not: I tell thee true.   105

CLOWN   Nay, I'll ne'er believe a madman till I see his brains. I
will fetch you light and paper and ink.

MALVOLIO   Fool, I' ll requite it in the highest degree. I prithee be
gone.

CLOWN   [*Sings.*]   I am gone, sir;   110

how did you lose your reason

91 Feste, as Sir Topas, makes a point of having the scholar-priest address himself as "good fellow" rather than "fool," as Malvolio and everyone else do. He also tells himself to go away again, so that Malvolio has to call out, as if the fool is his only lifeline to sanity.

misused, treated me as a thing

bully

consider

prattle

engage in
be with

reprimand

alas

103-09 Feste goes beyond Sir Toby's instructions in promising help, yet continues to push Malvolio towards further self-justification: this is what gives the fool most amusement. Lines 103-05 should probably be spoken so that "true," "mad," and "counterfeit" seem to lose all meaning as a result of Feste's efforts to gain Malvolio's admission of weakness and Malvolio's to gain Feste's serious attention. Their exchanges effect neither purpose but, if played intensely and in stillness, they can be heard by the audience as mottoes for the whole play: who can tell what is *"true"* when, in the speaker's own view, *"what is, is."* Alternatively, the exchange can be quick, absurd, heartless, and almost nonsensical.

Feste does not wait for Malvolio's reply to his last taunt (line 106), but promises help. Here the plot takes a significant step forward and, to mark this, the encounter between Feste and Malvolio is crowned by a song—a sign of its structural importance, for no other scene in this comedy terminates so strongly.

110-21 Feste's song (which seems to be an original composition, rather than a well-known one like others in the play) starts gaily but soon takes up the fiction that Malvolio is possessed by a devil who needs outrageous treatment. Feste probably imitates the behavior of a Vice from an old-fashioned interlude, with melodramatic gestures, loud cries, and a lot of energy. He gives a performance which is now like a jig, the grotesque and comic routine of song and dance that was customarily performed at the end of plays in Elizabethan theatres.

Malvolio makes no response, unless he cries out in renewed and inarticulate frustration (see his earlier cries of "fool," lines 68-72). Often Feste closes the trapdoor and dances in triumph on top of it.

Devils in old plays were often accompanied by smoke, fireworks, and thunder and these may well have been provided here. Today directors will sometimes supply thunder and the sounds of storms in such a way that they echo earlier representations of the storm at sea that had cast Viola,

And anon, sir,
I'll be with you again,
In a trice,
    Like to the old Vice,°
    Your need to sustain;°   115
Who with dagger of lath,
In his rage° and his wrath,°
    Cries "Ah ha" to the devil;
Like a mad lad,
"Pare thy nails,° dad."   120
    Adieu, goodman° devil.   *Exit.*

Scene iii   *Enter* SEBASTIAN.

SEBASTIAN   This is the air; that is the glorious sun;
This pearl she gave me, I do feel't, and see't:
And though 'tis wonder that enwraps me thus,
Yet 'tis not madness.—Where's Antonio then?
I could not find him at the Elephant;   5
Yet there he was,° and there I found this credit,°
That he did range the town to seek me out.
His counsel now might do me golden service;
For though my soul disputes well with my sense°
That this may be some error, but no madness,   10
Yet doth this accident° and flood of fortune
So far exceed all instance,° all discourse,°
That I am ready to distrust mine eyes,
And wrangle with my reason that persuades me
To any other trust° but that I am mad,   15
Or else the lady's mad.—Yet if 'twere so,
She could not sway° her house, command her followers,
Take and give back affairs and their dispatch°
With such a smooth, discreet, and stable bearing
As I perceive she does: there's something in't   20
That is deceivable.°—But here the lady comes.

(comic, mischievous character
in morality plays)
i.e., help you resist the devil

folly, passion   ardor

Sebastian, and Antonio ashore. By any of these means, the burlesque treatment of "rage," "wrath," and "madness" in Feste's song becomes associated with the play's other intimations of darkness and destruction beneath the appearances of life; it will also look forward to Feste's final song of the wind and the rain". What is certainly required by the text is a mimic fury and a relaxation from the immediate concerns of Malvolio, a change of mood to one in which more general and timeless significance can be suggested.

i.e., the devil's talons

mister

Scene iii

1-21   Sebastian enters dazed and happy, his mind racing to try to understand what has happened. As he speaks his first repetitive, half-line phrases, he is searching for something to steady his mind, looking as far off as the sun and as near as a pearl in his hand. Line 4 is split between reassurance and insecurity (or perhaps alarm), but in the long sentence of lines 9 to 16 Sebastian can hardly pause for breath if he is to make sense of all that he says. He stops as he thinks he is mad and, the next moment, thinks Olivia may be as well, or instead of himself. Fear mixes with happiness and incredulity, and with the evidence of his own eyes. He is so alert that he sees Olivia before she can speak or approach him.

had been   report

my very being argues with my
    reason

chance event

precedent   reasoning

belief

rule

be responsible for, and in com-
    mand of, business and man-
    agement

deceptive

Enter OLIVIA *and* PRIEST.

OLIVIA   Blame not this haste of mine:—if you mean well,
    Now go with me, and with this holy man,
    Into the chantry° by:° there, before him,
    And underneath that consecrated roof,   25
    Plight me the full assurance of your faith,°
    That my most jealous and too doubtful° soul
    May live at peace. He shall conceal it
    Whiles° you are willing it shall come to note,°
    What time we will our celebration° keep   30
    According to my birth.—What do you say?

SEBASTIAN   I'll follow this good man, and go with you;
    And having sworn truth, ever will be true.

OLIVIA   Then lead the way good father, and heavens so shine,
    That they may fairly note° this act of mine.   *Exeunt.*   35

chapel endowed for prayers
for the dead   nearby

i.e., become formally
betrothed
apprehensive

until   general knowledge
marriage ceremony

look with favor on

22   Olivia wastes no words before excusing her haste. The silent priest may be the *real* Sir Topas, so that the audience may wonder at first if it is Feste returning in disguise. However, the mere presence of this "holy man" (23) makes Olivia's purpose so unambiguous that it may be Shakespeare intended to raise a laugh here—one will come very easily in performance. The dignity and sensitivity of her following lines are liable, however, to silence any laughter, at least until "What do you say?" (31) eagerly forestalls Sebastian's reply.

32-33   Like the "mad" Malvolio at the climax to the previous scene (see IV.ii.105), Sebastian can only swear to be "true;" the difference is that he chooses his dream, or madness, quite deliberately now that he is again in the actual presence of Olivia.

34-35   Calling the heavens to "shine," Olivia provides another pointed contrast with the previous scene that had finished with a vice and devil at a dark prison. In place of a mad dance, Olivia and Sebastian walk offstage solemnly and lovingly, going to their formal betrothal. Sebastian speaks no more of madness and distrust.

ACT V

Scene i   *Enter* Clown *and* Fabian.

FABIAN   Now as thou lovest me, let me see his letter.

CLOWN   Good Master° Fabian, grant me another request.

FABIAN   Anything.

CLOWN   Do not desire to see this letter.

FABIAN   This is to give a dog, and in recompense desire my dog   5
again.

Enter Duke, Viola, Curio, *and* Lords.

DUKE   Belong you to the Lady Olivia, friends?

CLOWN   Ay sir, we are some of her trappings.

DUKE   I know thee well. How dost thou, my good fellow?

CLOWN   Truly sir, the better for my foes, and the worse for my   10
friends.

DUKE   Just the contrary: the better for thy friends.

CLOWN   No sir, the worse.

DUKE   How can that be?

CLOWN   Marry sir, they praise me, and make an ass of me.   15
Now my foes tell me plainly I am an ass; so that by my foes
sir, I profit in the knowledge of myself, and by my friends
I am abused;° so that, conclusions to be as kisses,° if your
four negatives make your two affirmatives,° why then, the
worse for my friends, and the better for my foes.   20

ACT V. Scene i

1-6 Feste answers Fabian's plea "as thou lovest me" with gentlemanly politeness, and then disappoints his ensuing trust; and so, on a joking and mocking level, the power of anyone to give or withhold is established at the beginning of the various meetings of the last scene. The letter is a quick and efficient reminder of what has happened to Malvolio.

(title of a gentleman, rather than a servant)

7-9 Orsino is now prepared to woo Olivia himself: "friends" and "good fellow" suggest a studied politeness, even to her servants and fool. (In II. iv, Orsino had called Feste, simply, "fellow.")

15-20 Feste delays Orsino—and dramatic development—to play another variation on what is and what is not: praise (or blame) is, he implies, only as it is received. Talk of "kisses" and "negatives" probably alludes obliquely to Orsino's presumed mission to Olivia.

deceived / insulted   (as when coy girls say *no* and mean *yes*)

i.e., as four lips make two kisses

DUKE   Why, this is excellent.

CLOWN   By my troth sir, no; though it please you to be one of my
friends.

DUKE   Thou shalt not be the worse for me,—there's gold.

CLOWN   But that it would be double-dealing° sir, I would you   25
could make it another.

DUKE   O you give me ill counsel.

CLOWN   Put your grace° in your pocket sir, for this once, and let
your flesh and blood obey it.°

DUKE   Well, I will be so much a sinner to be a double-dealer:—   30
there's another.

CLOWN   *Primo, secundo, tertio*° is a good play;° and the old saying is "The third pays for all." The triplex° sir, is a good
tripping measure;° or the bells of Saint Bennet° sir, may put
you in mind—one, two, three.   35

DUKE   You can fool no more money out of me at this throw.° If
you will let your lady know I am here to speak with her, and
bring her along with you, it may awake my bounty further.

CLOWN   Marry sir, lullaby to your bounty till I come again. I go   39
sir; but I would not have you to think that my desire of having
is the sin of covetousness. But, as you say sir, let your bounty
take a nap; I will awake it anon.   *Exit.*

> *Enter* ANTONIO *and* OFFICERS.

VIOLA   Here comes the man sir, that did rescue me.

DUKE   That face of his I do remember well;
Yet when I saw it last, it was besmeared   45
As black as Vulcan° in the smoke of war.
A baubling° vessel was he captain of,
For shallow draught and bulk unprizable,°
With which such scathful° grapple did he make,
With the most noble bottom° of our fleet,   50
That very envy and the tongue of loss
Cried fame and honor on him.° What's the matter?

21-23 Feste allows Orsino to be sure of nothing, except that he is expected to give a tip—a point he probably makes unmistakably by holding out his hand.

giving twice/duplicity

25-26, 28-29 Feste tries another trick as he sidles up to Orsino to ask confidentially that he should be indiscreet. Perhaps Feste's purpose is to get Orsino to play the fool and confess that he follows "ill counsel" and is a "double-dealer" in his pursuit of Olivia.

virtue/(hand of a) nobleman

i.e., the *ill counsel*

one, two, three   gamble, game
triple time (in music)
quantity/rhythm/dance
   church of St. Benedict

(of the dice)

36-42 For the first time, Orsino states his business. Shakespeare has risked the audience's impatience while establishing Orsino's new mood because only a very skillful actor of Feste can make this episode other than tedious and obscure. As Viola has said, the fool must "check at every feather" (see III.i.59) and improvise on whatever response he gets. Well played, the episode can be alert and wayward, suggesting quick-changing thoughts and a need for some kind of mutual agreement—an appropriate preparation as the play draws towards its final confrontations.

43-58 Viola's one-line speech makes it almost certain that Antonio will think that he sees Sebastian immediately on his entry. He will stand amazed and yet further appalled by his friend's apparent friendship with his own great enemy. Some Antonios struggle with the guards to approach Viola, but there is nothing in the text that implies this.

Roman god of fire and smiths
ridiculously small and lively
not worth capturing
damaging
vessel

absolute enemies and victims
   both acclaim his renown
   and honor

FIRST OFFICER   Orsino, this is that Antonio
 That took the Phoenix and her fraught° from Candy;°
 And this is he that did the Tiger board   55
 When your young nephew Titus lost his leg.
 Here in the streets, desperate° of shame and state,°
 In private brabble° did we apprehend him.

VIOLA   He did me kindness sir, drew on my side;°
 But in conclusion put strange speech upon me.°   60
 I know not what 'twas but distraction.°

DUKE   Notable pirate, thou salt-water thief,
 What foolish boldness brought thee to their mercies
 Whom thou in terms° so bloody and so dear°
 Hast made thine enemies?

ANTONIO   Orsino, noble sir,   65
 Be pleased that I shake off these names you give me:
 Antonio never yet was thief, or pirate,
 Though I confess, on base and ground enough,
 Orsino's enemy. A witchcraft drew me hither:
 That most ingrateful boy, there, by your side,   70
 From the rude sea's enraged and foamy mouth
 Did I redeem°—a wreck past hope he was—
 His life I gave him, and did thereto add
 My love without retention or restraint,
 All his in dedication. For his sake   75
 Did I expose myself (pure° for his love)
 Into the danger of this adverse° town;
 Drew to defend him when he was beset;
 Where being apprehended, his false cunning
 (Not meaning to partake with me in danger)   80
 Taught him to face me out of his acquaintance,°
 And grew a twenty years removèd° thing
 While one would wink; denied me mine own purse,
 Which I had recommended° to his use
 Not half an hour before.

VIOLA   How can this be?   85

DUKE   When came he to this town?

ANTONIO   Today, my lord; and for three months before,

cargo   Crete

careless   good order
brawl

drew his sword in my defense
spoke strangely to me
unless it were madness

59-61   Antonio will be further dismayed by Viola's easy talk of "kindness". If he makes a strong audible or physical reaction, it will be obvious that Viola cannot yet inquire after Sebastian. However, if Orsino moves forward to question Antonio, Viola will move with him (see line 70) and so be more ready to do so.

manner   grievous/costly

69-75   As the "notable" sea captain talks of "witchcraft," "love," and "dedication", Orsino's attention is directed to Viola whose face and bearing will deny, and then affirm, what is spoken, and then deny it again. The parenthetical line 80 calls for scornful delivery, and so do "thing" and "wink." Antonio probably speaks with such a rising passion that no interruption is possible; to Orsino, what he says sounds like "madness" (see line 91).

recover

merely/purely
unfriendly

deny to my face that he knew
     me
separated

entrusted

86-89   Orsino's question touches the nub of the misunderstandings and, after a pause directed by a half-line of verse, Antonio's certainty in reply marks this clearly. His "we," delayed until line 89, is a direct

No int'rim, not a minute's vacancy,
Both day and night did we keep company.

Enter OLIVIA *and* ATTENDANTS.

DUKE   Here comes the countess; now heaven walks on earth.   90
But for thee, fellow: fellow, thy words are madness.
Three months this youth hath tended upon me;
But more of that anon. Take him aside.

OLIVIA   What would my lord, but that° he may not have,
Wherein Olivia may seem serviceable?°   95
Cesario, you do not keep promise with me.

VIOLA   Madam?

DUKE   Gracious Olivia . . .

OLIVIA   What do you say, Cesario?—Good my lord°—

VIOLA   My lord would speak; my duty hushes me.   100

OLIVIA   If it be aught to the old tune, my lord,
It is as fat and fulsome° to mine ear
As howling after music.

DUKE   Still so cruel?

OLIVIA   Still so constant, lord.

DUKE   What! to perverseness? You uncivil lady,   105
To whose ingrate and unauspicious° altars
My soul the faithfull'st off'rings have breathed out
That e'er devotion tendered. What shall I do?

OLIVIA   Even what it please my lord, that shall become him.

DUKE   Why should I not, had I the heart to do it,   110
Like to th' Egyptian thief° at point of death,
Kill what I love?—a savage jealousy
That sometime savors nobly. But hear me this:
Since you to non-regardance° cast my faith,°
And that I partly know the instrument   115
That screws° me from my true place in your favor,
Live you the marble-breasted tyrant still.
But this your minion,° whom I know you love,

challenge to Viola so that they must now look each other in the eye, for confirmation or denial. Shakespeare, however, still holds back full recognition by directing Olivia to enter at this precise moment.

90-95   Orsino may well be amazed that Olivia has not refused to see him: her presence is like a miracle or ancient myth. As she approaches, he puts the question of what to do about Antonio on hold.

that which (i.e., my love)

willing to be of service

Olivia may curtsy to Orsino, but her words, though sweetly reasonable, show that she is preoccupied with her new relationship to Sebastian—with what she no longer has to give.

96-7   Olivia now speaks directly to Viola as to her husband of a few hours. Viola's response can be an unguarded exclamation or a reproof; it will follow or precede a silence.

i.e., please be silent (so Cesario
  may speak)

gross and repulsive

104   This line can be careful, firm, and respectful; or it can be defiant and strong, followed by a movement and smile towards Viola, inviting a contrary understanding—this reading would explain Orsino's "uncivil" at line 105.

ungrateful and unpropitious

(Thyramis, from Greek novel
  Ethiopica: in darkness he
  killed the wrong woman)

disregard*   true love

wrenches

darling

110-24   Orsino speaks wildly at first, ready to commit murder, but then with growing assurance, strength, and subdued anger. When he speaks of Cesario, as Olivia's "minion," his rhythms become even more disturbed than before, and then strengthen as he again is ready for violent murder of the (supposed) boy. He is well aware of the danger of his reactions and tender enough toward his new victim to speak (like Othello) of "sacrifice," rather than of killing and savage jealousy as at line 112, above.

And whom, by heaven I swear, I tender° dearly,
Him will I tear out of that cruel eye   120
Where he sits crowned° in his master's spite.°
Come boy, with me; my thoughts are ripe in mischief:
I'll sacrifice the lamb that I do love
To spite a raven's heart within a dove.   [*Going.*]

VIOLA   And I, most jocund, apt,° and willingly,   125
To do you rest,° a thousand deaths would die.   [*Following.*]

OLIVIA   Where goes Cesario?

VIOLA   After him I love
More than I love these eyes, more than my life,
More, by all mores,° than e'er I shall love wife.
If I do feign, you witnesses above,   130
Punish my life for tainting of my love!

OLIVIA   Ay me detested,° how am I beguiled!°

VIOLA   Who does beguile you? Who does do you wrong?

OLIVIA   Hast thou forgot thyself? Is it so long?
Call forth the holy father.   [*Exit an* ATTENDANT.]

DUKE   [*To* VIOLA.]   Come away.   135

OLIVIA   Whither my lord? Cesario, husband, stay.

DUKE   Husband?

OLIVIA   Ay, husband. Can he that deny?

DUKE   Her husband, sirrah?°

VIOLA   No my lord, not I.

OLIVIA   Alas, it is the baseness of thy fear
That makes thee strangle thy propriety.°   140
Fear not Cesario; take thy fortunes up;
Be that thou know'st thou art, and then thou art
As great as that° thou fear'st.

                        Enter PRIEST.

                        O welcome, father!
Father, I charge thee by thy reverence

care for

(lover is imagined to be mir-
    rored in his lady's eye)
  in defiance of his master

prepared

give you peace

125-26   Some Violas say these lines fearfully or
regretfully; others far more lightly, being aware of the
sexual meanings commonly given to *die* and making
the most of the selfless concern that is implied in "do
you rest" In a broadly comic production at the outdoor
Delacorte Theatre in Central Park, New York, Mary
Elizabeth Mastrantonio as Viola, "her tears of longing
still gleaming in her wide eyes, leaps on [Orsino's]
back to celebrate the long-delayed reciprocation of
her affections" (*New York Times*, 10 July, 1989).

i.e., possible comparisons

detestable   cheated

127   Olivia's three words must have sufficient
power of surprise, outrage, pain, or incomprehension
to stop the others from leaving the stage.

135   With "Come away" Orsino may sustain his
murderous intentions or, somewhat less violently, be
pulling Viola away from Olivia's excessive (and
potentially comic) attentions.

(address to a menial)

136   Olivia is desperate and breaks her promise
of secrecy in using the word "husband." To everyone
on stage, the effect is explosive and causes a nearly
total disorientation. They stop in their tracks as they
were about to leave and all turn towards Olivia, and
then towards Viola who is now, at first, amazedly
silent.

suppress your true identity (as
    husband)

i.e., the Duke

138-48   The phrasing of Viola's response—with
"not I" as a neat conclusion—is often taken as an
invitation to speak it fearfully and comically. But it can
be more emphatic, expressing a (secret) delight in
the dismissal of one confusion and the opening of a
way back into Orsino's affection. Olivia interrupts to
interpret any denial as due to "fear", her threefold use
of this word suggesting her own insecurity. She turns
to the priest just as soon as he enters.

Here to unfold—though lately we intended   145
To keep in darkness what occasion° now
Reveals before 'tis ripe—what thou dost know
Hath newly passed,° between this youth and me.

PRIEST   A contract° of eternal bond of love,
    Confirmed by mutual joinder of your hands,   150
    Attested by the holy close° of lips,
    Strength'ned by interchangement of your rings;
    And all the ceremony of this compact
    Sealed in my function,° by my testimony;
    Since when, my watch hath told me, toward my grave   155
    I have traveled but two hours.

DUKE   O thou dissembling cub! What wilt thou be
    When time hath sowed a grizzle on thy case?°
    Or will not else thy craft° so quickly grow
    That thine own trip° shall be thine overthrow?   160
    Farewell, and take her; but direct thy feet
    Where thou and I, henceforth, may never meet.

VIOLA   My lord, I do protest . . .

OLIVIA   O do not swear.
    Hold little° faith, though thou hast too much fear.

Enter SIR ANDREW.

SIR ANDREW   For the love of God, a surgeon! Send one pres-   165
    ently° to Sir Toby.

OLIVIA   What's the matter?

SIR ANDREW   H' as broke my head across, and has given Sir
    Toby a bloody coxcomb° too: for the love of God, your help!
    I had rather than forty pound I were at home.   170

OLIVIA   Who has done this, Sir Andrew?

SIR ANDREW   The count's gentleman, one Cesario. We took him
    for a coward, but he's the very devil incardinate.°

DUKE   My gentleman Cesario?

SIR ANDREW   Od's lifelings,° here he is! You broke my head for   175

personal need, course of
events

transacted

betrothal

149-56 The priest's words introduce a new rhythm, each line fully laden and its sense running to its full length. He says all that is necessary in his first line and then proceeds to elaborate. He sounds firm, untroubled, and even otherworldly (an effect made explicit in his last two lines and his complete silence for the rest of the play).

union, meeting

office as a priest

gray hairs on your outside (or
mask)
deceit/occupation
false step/throw (in wrestling)

163 Viola is desperate and about to reveal all, but Shakespeare for the second time holds back disclosures by means of Olivia's interruption and Sir Andrew's entry with a bloody and roughly bandaged head—he may cry out in pain while still offstage and so build up the effect of this re-entry.

a little

immediately

head/fool's hat

(blunder for *incarnate*, in the
flesh)

174, 175-76 On the duke's cue, everyone will look at Viola while a fearful Sir Andrew may try to hide in a box tree. His fear is redoubled and, instead of boasting of Sir Toby's company, he now blames his friend for what he has suffered.

by God's life

nothing; and that that I did, I was set on to do't by Sir Toby.

VIOLA   Why do you speak to me? I never hurt, you:
You drew your sword upon me without cause,
But I bespake you fair and hurt you not.

Enter SIR TOBY *and* CLOWN.

SIR ANDREW   If a bloody coxcomb be a hurt, you have hurt me.   180
I think you set nothing by° a bloody coxcomb. Here comes
Sir Toby halting;° you shall hear more. But if he had not been
in drink, he would have tickled you othergates° than he did.

DUKE   How now, gentleman? How is't with you?

SIR TOBY   That's all one! H' as hurt me, and there's th' end on't.   185
Sot,° didst see Dick Surgeon, sot?

CLOWN   O he's drunk, Sir Toby, an hour agone. His eyes were
set° at eight i' th' morning.

SIR TOBY   Then he's a rogue, and a passy measures pavin.° I hate
a drunken rogue.   190

OLIVIA   Away with him! Who hath made this havoc with them?

SIR ANDREW   I'll help you, Sir Toby, because we'll be dressed°
together.

SIR TOBY   Will you help—an ass-head, and a coxcomb, and a
knave, a thin-faced knave, a gull?°   195

OLIVIA   Get him to bed, and let his hurt be looked to.
        [*Exeunt* CLOWN, FABIAN, SIR TOBY *and* SIR ANDREW.]

Enter SEBASTIAN.

SEBASTIAN   I am sorry, madam, I have hurt your kinsman;
But had it been the brother of my blood,
I must have done no less with wit and safety.°
You throw a strange regard° upon me, and by that   200
I do perceive it hath offended you.
Pardon me, sweet one, even for the vows
We made each other but so late° ago.

think nothing of
limping
otherwise

180-83 Again, with Sir Toby's entry, Shakespeare has brought in another character instead of allowing Viola to disclose her identity. Sir Toby's presence encourages Sir Andrew to be somewhat bolder.

fool/drunkard

closed

passamezzo pavane (slow, state-
ly dance in sections of eight
bars each)

have our wounds dressed

dupe

185-96 This is Sir Toby's only appearance in Act V and so the actor will seek the most effective treat-ment of his very few words in order to make a strong last impression. However, much can also be con-veyed by his silences, including, perhaps, a refusal to answer Olivia who, as mistress of the house, would expect to be addressed.

The shame of his offstage defeat means that the knight is rendered speechless until Orsino puts two questions to him, which he brushes aside preferring to talk with the fool. It is hard to know whether he is now accepting removal from polite society or trying to behave as if such concerns did not exist; perhaps he attempts both. In what he does say, anger and self-reproach can color every word as he insults first the absent surgeon and then Sir Andrew who is offering to help. At Stratford-upon-Avon in 1988, "'I hate a drunken rogue' [was] deliv-ered straight to his patroness as a plea not to throw him out of the house" (*Times*). When Olivia does speak, it is about Sir Toby and not addressed to him, as if she wishes to separate herself from him.

Most Sir Andrews delay their exit to emphasize their distress at being dismissed by Sir Toby; sometimes he leaves the stage weeping or in a {delayed} panic.

taking thought for my safety
unfriendly look

recently

197-213 Sebastian appears unheralded where the two knights had just entered and immediately com-mands attention and maintains it in the face of blank astonishment. He is full of his own business with Olivia and so does not see Viola until line 210. Orsino's "that is, and is not" echoes what the fool has said earlier (see IV.i.7, IV.ii.13-15) and he must say it with sufficient emphasis to take Sebastian's attention so that he turns and sees Antonio. Expressing con-

DUKE   One face, one voice, one habit,° and two persons—
    A natural perspective,° that is, and is not.   205

SEBASTIAN   Antonio, O my dear Antonio,
    How have the hours racked and tortured me
    Since I have lost thee!

ANTONIO   Sebastian are you?

SEBASTIAN   Fear'st thou° that, Antonio?

ANTONIO   How have you made division of yourself?   210
    An apple cleft in two is not more twin
    Than these two creatures. Which is Sebastian?

OLIVIA   Most wonderful.

SEBASTIAN   Do I stand there? I never had a brother;
    Nor can there be that deity in my nature   215
    Of here and everywhere.° I had a sister,
    Whom the blind waves and surges have devoured:—
    Of charity,° what kin are you to me?
    What countryman? What name? What parentage?

VIOLA   Of Messaline: Sebastian was my father;   220
    Such a Sebastian was my brother too,
    So went he suited° to his watery tomb.
    If spirits can assume both form and suit,°
    You come to fright us.

SEBASTIAN   A spirit I am indeed,
    But am in that dimension grossly clad   225
    Which from the womb I did participate.°
    Were you a woman, as the rest goes even,°
    I should my tears let fall upon your cheek,
    And say, "Thrice welcome, drownèd Viola!"

VIOLA   My father had a mole upon his brow.   230

SEBASTIAN   And so had mine.

VIOLA   And died that day when Viola from her birth
    Had numb'red thirteen years.

SEBASTIAN   O that record° is lively in my soul!
    He finished indeed his mortal act   235

dress

lifelike optical illusion

cern for him with stronger words than ever before, Sebastian amazes Antonio who now pauses before replying with an incredulous question. This and his extended simile of the apple do something to halt the audience's laughter that will easily arise in the scene of general amazement. Following Antonio's direction question, Olivia's "Most wonderful!" can be rapt, or thankful, or coquettish, or, even, apprehensive. Inevitably, however spoken, these two words can cause laughter more easily than any great intensity

do you doubt

of feeling. Everyone on stage is caught in perplexity, except Viola who is notably silent until she speaks with quiet confidence and joy.

220-24   Viola does not rush into Sebastian's arms, as realism might suggest, nor does she answer his questions at once. Rather she answers slowly and carefully, so that she seems to be remembering her childhood, her father's death, and her hope that her brother was not drowned. Her very first words can speak for the depth of her engagement: "As

nor can I, like a god, be in more than one place at a time

out of simple kindness

Sebastian faces his sister there is a long pause before Viola in almost a whisper (but one of infinite rapture and astonishment) answers: 'Of Messaline'… Viola has forced me to believe in her past: in that rapt pause Peggy Ashcroft speaks the whole story of Viola's despairs, longings and hopes" (J. C. Trewin, *John O'London's,* 8 December 1950).

Lines 223-24 show that an uncanny fear should also be part of her reaction, and her first short phrases, followed by "Such," "too," and "So," can also express this powerfully. Viola is holding on with trepidation to the new reality that has just appeared before her; she is taking her first steps towards happiness.

dressed

body and clothing

224-29   Sebastian's curious way of talking (especially lines 225-6) suggests a clumsy humor as a defense against too sudden a shock—as a kind of wariness. He is close to weeping for joy (see line 228). He was less prepared for the recognition than Viola, who knew already that her twin was alive and close at hand, but he seems the more eager of the two to embrace (see Viola's caution at lines 239-41).

clothed in that fleshly body
    which I inherited from birth

agrees with

230-33   Viola probably restrains Sebastian from embracing her by this recounting of further details. A pause before or after his reply, and also after line 233, can suggest that both are now thinking and acting together so that they share in silences as well as words. They speak slowly and deliberately in order to contain the rush of sudden happiness that they experience in remembering past intimacy and sharing past sorrow.

memory

That day that made my sister thirteen years.

VIOLA   If nothing lets° to make us happy both
But this my masculine usurped° attire,
Do not embrace me till each circumstance
Of place, time, fortune do cohere and jump°   240
That I am Viola; which to confirm,
I'll bring you to a captain in this town,
Where lie my maiden weeds;° by whose gentle help
I was preserved to serve this noble count.
All the occurrence of my fortune since   245
Hath been between this lady, and this lord.

SEBASTIAN   [*To* OLIVIA.] So comes it, lady, you have been mistook:
But nature to her bias drew° in that.
You would have been contracted to a maid;°
Nor are you therein, by my life, deceived: 250
You are betrothed both to a maid° and man.

DUKE   Be not amazed; right noble is his blood.
If this be so, as yet the glass° seems true,
I shall have share in this most happy wreck.
[*To* VIOLA.] Boy, thou hast said to me a thousand times   255
Thou never shouldst love woman like to me.

VIOLA   And all those sayings will I overswear,°
And all those swearings keep as true in soul
As doth that orbèd continent° the fire
That severs day from night.

DUKE   Give me thy hand,   260
And let me see thee in thy woman's weeds.

VIOLA   The captain that did bring me first on shore
Hath my maid's garments. He upon some action
Is now in durance, at Malvolio's suit,°
A gentleman, and follower of my lady's.   265

OLIVIA   He shall enlarge° him. Fetch Malvolio hither—
And yet alas, now I remember me,
They say, poor gentleman, he's much distract.°

Enter CLOWN *with a letter, and* FABIAN.

hinders

false

agree

237-46 As the recognition and recollection are completed, Sebastian moves to embrace his sister but Viola stops him and completes her story; this widens the audience's attention once more, to include both Olivia and Orsino.

dress

followed her normal inclination

girl

247-51 Now comedy is explicit in "mistook" and the pun on "maid": easy laughter joins with amazement, relaxing the mood.

virgin

i.e., the *natural perspective*, line 205

swear over again

sphere of the sun

255 Orsino calls Viola "Boy" for the first time since he has known her true sex. This may suggest an uneasiness half-hidden in a new and happy capacity for wit and laughter; or it might be a way of recognizing the "love" (see line 123) he had already felt for Cesario (and which is the strongest anchor of his feelings now that his fantasies about Olivia have been destroyed). Either way, the word *Boy* initiates Orsino's wooing of Viola.

257-61 Orsino's first four words contrast with Viola's surging rhythms and cosmic imagery. They suggest that the two touch, very simply, as man and woman for the first time: in some productions it is the first time they have actually made physical contact with each other although drawn several times into close intimacy. (The text nowhere earlier insists physical contact.)

at Malvolio's instigation he is now imprisoned on some legal charge

release

mad

A most extracting° frenzy of mine own
From my remembrance clearly banished his.   270
How does he, sirrah?

CLOWN   Truly madam, he holds Belzebub at the stave's end° as
well as a man in his case° may do. Has here writ a letter to you;
I should have given't you today morning. But as a madman's
epistles are no gospels, so it skills° not much when they are
delivered.   276

OLIVIA   Open't, and read it.

CLOWN   Look then to be well edified, when the fool delivers°
the madman. [*Reads in a mad voice.*] "By the lord, madam . . ."

OLIVIA   How now! Art thou mad?   280

CLOWN   No madam, I do but read madness. And your ladyship
will have it as it ought to be, you must allow *vox.* °

OLIVIA   Prithee read i' thy right wits.

CLOWN   So I do, madonna; but to read his right wits is to read
thus. Therefore perpend,° my princess, and give ear.   285

OLIVIA   [*To* FABIAN.]   Read it you, sirrah.

FABIAN   [*Reads.*]   "By the lord, madam, you wrong me, and the
world shall know it. Though you have put me into darkness, and given your drunken cousin rule over me, yet have I
the benefit of my senses as well as your ladyship. I have your
own letter that induced me to the semblance I put on; with the
which I doubt not but to do myself much right, or you much
shame. Think of me as you please. I leave my duty a little un-
thought of, and speak out of my injury.
                          THE MADLY USED MALVOLIO."   295

OLIVIA   Did he write this?

CLOWN   Ay, madam.

DUKE   This savors not much of distraction.

OLIVIA   See him delivered, Fabian; bring him hither.
                                                 [*Exit* FABIAN.]
My lord, so please you, these things further thought on,   300
To think me as well a sister as a wife,

obliterating* (wordplay on *distract.* line 268)

i.e., keeps the devil at a dis-
    tance
    condition

matters

272-85   Feste reads Malvolio's letter giving a performance of a priest reading the Epistle in a church
service (see line 275): so he mocks Malvolio's presumption and shows his own delight in disguises. His
onstage audience does not know where the "madness" lies (280-81) and, yet again, events are held up
by perplexity about what is and is not.

(pun on reading the set
    Epistles and *Gospels* for each
    day)

i.e., the appropriate voice

consider (mock pedantic)

287   Fabian at last gets the letter he had asked
for at the beginning of the scene. He makes no comment and neither does Feste, but most actors add
some by-play to remind the audience of this small
victory. The reading of someone else's letter, especially one so full of "I," "me," and "my," requires a very
different delivery from the intense, happy, zany, and
direct talk that has preceded it. So the audience is
encouraged to give a simpler and, perhaps, more
judicial or "alienated" attention in which Malvolio's
elaborate elaborate self-justification can register
coldly and clearly.

300-03   Olivia has completely recovered the
"smooth, discreet and stable bearing" that Sebastian
had noted (see IV.iii.19).

One day shall crown th' alliance on't, so please you,
Here at my house and at my proper° cost.

DUKE   Madam, I am most apt° t' embrace your offer.
    [*To* VIOLA.] Your master quits° you; and for your service
        done him,   305
    So much against the mettle of your sex,
    So far beneath your soft and tender breeding,
    And since you called me master for so long,
    Here is my hand; you shall from this time be
    Your master's mistress.

OLIVIA   A sister; you are she.   310

            Enter [FABIAN, *with*] MALVOLIO.

DUKE   Is this the madman?

OLIVIA   Ay my lord, this same.
    How now, Malvolio?

MALVOLIO   Madam, you have done me wrong,
    Notorious wrong.

OLIVIA   Have I, Malvolio? No.

MALVOLIO   Lady, you have. Pray you peruse that letter.
    You must not now deny it is your hand.   315
    Write from it° if you can, in hand or phrase,
    Or say 'tis not your seal, not your invention:
    You can say none of this. Well, grant it then,
    And tell me, in the modesty of honor,°
    Why you have given me such clear lights° of favor,   320
    Bade me come smiling and cross-gartered to you,
    To put on yellow stockings, and to frown
    Upon Sir Toby and the lighter° people;
    And, acting this in an obedient hope,
    Why have you suffered me to be imprisoned,   325
    Kept in a dark house, visited by the priest,
    And made the most notorious geck° and gull.
    That e'er invention played on? Tell me why.

OLIVIA   Alas Malvolio, this is not my writing,
    Though I confess much like the character;°   330

own

ready

frees

differently

with proper respect for your
own honor

indications

less important

fool

handwriting

304-10 Orsino probably embraces Olivia and kisses her. When he turns back to Viola, he may speak at first to the wrong "boy," mistaking Sebastian for his sister.

At line 310, Orsino possibly kneels to Viola, thus completing the change from master to servant—with a touch, perhaps, of conscious playacting that would be appropriate to Twelfth Night revels.

310 Olivia's "you are she" suggests that she makes a point of recognizing the right twin. She probably embraces Viola as Malvolio is about to enter.

312-28 Malvolio enters from his imprisonment physically transformed: blear-eyed, unkempt, stripped of his doublet, his garters hanging down. He sees Olivia with Cesario and Orsino, both rivals for his lady's love, and he also sees two Cesarios: for him, it is a strange world but, at first, he says nothing of all this, simply holding in his hand the letter that is evidence for believing his fantasies. He is obsessed by the wrong he has suffered and his own blamelessness; in his wretchedness, therefore, he holds himself erect.

At first silent, he then answers a question with few words. When Olivia denies his charge, he delivers himself of a sustained speech moving from premise to deduction and then to interrogation, and speaking with the unbroken certainty that he has done all correctly. If Malvolio has been played as a very intelligent man misled by his own egotism, ambition, and fantasies, the speech might, perhaps, be spoken as a brilliant improvisation. For most Malvolios, it is a carefully prepared and memorized vindication, spoken with great feeling that is controlled only by an equally great effort.

329-31 To Olivia's revelation, Malvolio says nothing. In some productions, he cries out in pain, while the onlookers laugh; in other productions, he barely understands at first and makes a move to take back the letter; or he understands and still resolves to vindicate himself or to bear the affront silently; or he looks around in anger for Maria. Olivia, however, continues to explain and then to sympathize, so that Malvolio's predicament does not yet take full attention.

But, out of question, 'tis Maria's hand.
And now I do bethink me, it was she
First told me thou wast mad; then cam'st in smiling,
And in such forms which here were presupposed
Upon thee in the letter. Prithee be content;   335
This practice° hath most shrewdly° passed° upon thee.
But when we know the grounds and authors of it;
Thou shalt be both the plaintiff and the judge
Of thine own cause.

FABIAN   Good madam, hear me speak,
And let no quarrel, nor no brawl to come,   340
Taint the condition of this present hour,
Which I have wond'red at. In hope it shall not,
Most freely I confess myself and Toby
Set this device against Malvolio here,
Upon some stubborn and uncourteous parts°   345
We had conceived° against him. Maria writ
The letter, at Sir Toby's great importance,°
In recompense whereof he hath married her.
How with a sportful malice it was followed,
May rather pluck° on laughter than revenge,   350
If that the injuries be justly weighed,
That have on both sides passed.

OLIVIA   Alas, poor fool, how have they baffled° thee!

CLOWN   Why, "some are born great, some achieve greatness,
and some have greatness thrown upon them." I was one,   355
sir, in this interlude,° one Sir Topas, sir; but that's all one.
"By the Lord, fool, I am not mad!" But do you remember,
"Madam, why laugh you at such a barren rascal? And you
smile not, he's gagged?" And thus the whirligig° of time
brings in his revenges.   360

MALVOLIO   I'll be revenged on the whole pack of you!   [*Exit.*]

OLIVIA   He hath been most notoriously abused.

DUKE   Pursue him and entreat him to a peace.
He hath not told us of the captain yet.
When that is known, and golden time convents,°   365
A solemn combination shall be made

339-53 Fabian completes a verse-line of Olivia's, allowing no pause for Malvolio to reply. His speech does finish with an incomplete verse-line, indicating a pause in which he holds the stage in silence; in that time, an audience will sense Malvolio's determined refusal to believe what he has been told, or some shred of dignity, deep suffering, or, possibly, comic frustration. Again it is Olivia who speaks next, calling Malvolio a "baffled" fool—not the "madman" that Orsino had expected at line 311.

trick   sorely   passed
sentence

354-60 Feste's quotation of the letter that Malvolio has so often quoted will sting his remembrance. Feste continues lightly, and even politely, to remind him of his suffering and folly. Probably the whole speech should be spoken quietly, with Feste remaining in an onlooker's position.

361 Malvolio speaks after a long silence; he also has to cross the stage and exit. This is the actor's opportunity to sum up his whole performance, with the audience's attention closely fixed on him, waiting for the long-delayed response. He may speak before or after he moves, before or after a pause, quietly or loudly, to himself or to his enemies, or to the whole world: these are very important choices for the actor.

because of some rude and discourteous actions
held
urging

Henry Irving played the "madly used" steward "as an Italian who can be, when fully roused by injustice, as vindictive as Shylock...and as implacable as Othello...When he is released, it is with no bated breath that he dwells upon his wrongs...He does not slink from the stage a baffled and gulled simpleton...Stung to fury by the insolent quips and quiddities of the fool, the evil will of the steward makes itself, with terrific force, manifest. 'I'll be revenged on the whole pack of you' he screams, rather than exclaims, as he rushes from the stage. When an Italian by the name of Malvolio vows that he will take vengeance on his enemies, it is clear that he means mischief...Olivia begins to be frightened" (*Illustrated London News,* 12 July, 1884).

draw

publicly disgraced

early form of dramatic entertainment

whipping top

In contrast, John Gielgud's "sere and yellow Malvolio, Puritan to the core,...snarled his spiteful exit" (*Observer,* 7January,1931). Laurence Olivier made the words the natural, pained assertion of a "man who refuses to see himself as others see him" (*Shakespeare: A Celebration,* 1964, p. 82).

362-63 Olivia and Orsino speak in close accord. Olivia, however, quotes Malvolio's own words (compare 313, above, and IV.ii.80) and so she may suggest a greater sympathy or, alternately, use an edge of irony or humor.

summons/is convenient

Of our dear souls. Meantime, sweet sister,
We will not part from hence. Cesario, come—
For so you shall be while you are a man,
But when in other habits° you are seen,   370
Orsino's mistress, and his fancy's° queen.

                          Exeunt [all but the CLOWN.]

CLOWN   [*Sings.*] When that I was and a little tiny boy,
                With hey, ho, the wind and the rain,
            A foolish thing was but a toy,
                For the rain it raineth every day.   375

            But when I came to man's estate,
                With hey, ho, the wind and the rain,
            'Gainst knaves and thieves men shut their gate,
                For the rain it raineth every day.

            But when I came, alas, to wive,   380
                With hey, ho, the wind and the rain,
            By swaggering° could I never thrive,
                For the rain it raineth every day.

            But when I came unto my beds,
                With hey, ho, the wind and the rain,   385
            With tosspots° still had drunken heads,
                For the rain it raineth every day.

            A great while ago the world begun,
                Hey, ho, the wind and the rain;
            But that's all one, our play is done,   390
                And we'll strive to please you every day.

                                                              [*Exit.*]

                              FINIS

368   When Orsino turns to Cesario he may have to distinguish yet again between the twins; in many productions he does so consciously, and passes the test with happy success. The use of the name "Cesario" suggests that Shakespeare still wished to play upon the ambiguities of the disguise.

clothes
love's

372   The stage empties without any verbal response to Orsino: the characters must all wait for "golden time" (365) to convert words and fancies to reality. But Feste is left behind and nothing in his song suggests he has been watching the others leave. Usually he has sat still and unnoticed until he starts to sing: he is then seen to have been staring out into the distance.

The song brings a contrasting, wide view of the whole course of man's life and of the need for a generous, guiltless, and free acceptance of all things. It would be appropriate, after the other false voices he has assumed, for Feste to start singing childishly, or at least with a little voice, and later change to an older, more experienced mood.

boasting, bullying

Behind the isolated Feste at Stratford-upon-Avon in 1979, the various lovers could be seen walking slowly together and, seated at the sides of the large stage, "the wounded Aguecheek, head in hands, the isolated Antonio, and the sobered Maria and Toby, separated and facing away from each other" (*Shakespeare Survey*, 33, 1980).

drunkards

388-91   The last stanza, or the last two lines, will be addressed to the audience, inviting acceptance and applause.

Textual Notes

The text printed in the 1623 Folio is the sole authority. It was probably set from the actors' promptbook, or a transcript of it. Certainly it was an unusually clean manuscript, but some oaths may have been expurgated. In the following collation, all substansive changes from the Folio other than obvious misprints are recorded; the reading of the present edition is followed by that of the Folio.

I.iii.   87 *curl by* coole my   118 *dun colored* dam'd colour'd   121 *That's* That

II.ii.   17 *That sure* That   28 *our* O   29 *of* if
II.iii.   120 *a nayword* an ayword
II.iv.   51 *Fly...fly* Fye...fie   85 *I cannot* It cannot
II.v.   104 *staniel* stallion   129 *born* become; *acheive* atcheeues

III.i.   62 *wise men, folly-fall'n* wisemens folly falne
III.ii.   7 *see thee the* see the   56 *nine* mine
III.iii.   15 *ever thanks; and oft* euer oft
III.iv.   23 *OLIVIA* Mal.   64 *tang* langer   80 *SIR TOBY* [speech-prefix omitted in Folio]

IV.ii.   64 *to the upshot* the vppeshot

V.i.   189 *pavin* panyn   372 *tiny* tine

John Russell Brown

Editor and Commentary, *12th Night*,

General Editor Applause Shakespeare Library:

John Russell Brown has been a fellow of the Shakespeare Institute, Stratford upon Avon, the first head of the Dept of Drama and Theatre Arts at the Dept of Drama in Birminghnam (UK) and an Associate Director fo the Royal National Theatre. In the US he has taught at Coumbia University and the University of Michigan he has written about plays, acting and theatre and directed many plays in the UK and the US. Among his books that are available through Applause are: *Free Shakespeare*, *Shakespeare's Plays in Performance* and *Shakescenes*. His new book *Shakespeare: The Tragedies* will be published in February 2001.

SHAKESPEARE'S PLAYS IN PERFORMANCE by John Russell Brown

In this volume, John Russell Brown snatches Shakespeare from the clutches of dusty academics and thrusts him centerstage where he belongs—in performance.

Brown's thorough analysis of the theatrical experience of Shakespeare forcibly demonstrates how the text is brought to life: awakened, colored, emphasized, and extended by actors and audiences, designers and directors.

"A knowledge of what precisely can and should happen when a play is performed is, for me, the essential first step towards an understanding of Shakespeare."
—*from the Introduction by John Russell Brown*

paper•ISBN 1-55783-136-X•

SOLILOQUY!

The Shakespeare Monologues
Edited by Michael Earley and Philippa Keil

At last, over 175 of Shakespeare's finest and most performable monologues taken from all 37 plays are here in two easy-to-use volumes (MEN and WOMEN). Selections travel the entire spectrum of the great dramatist's vision, from comedies and romances to tragedies, pathos and histories.

"Soliloquy is an excellent and comprehensive collection of Shakespeare's speeches. Not only are the monologues wide-ranging and varied, but they are superbly annotated. Each volume is prefaced by an informative and reassuring introduction, which explains the signals and signposts by which Shakespeare helps an actor on his journey through the text. It includes a very good explanation of blank verse, with excellent examples of irregularities which are specifically related to character and acting intentions. These two books are a must for any actor in search of a 'classical' audition piece."

ELIZABETH SMITH
Head of Voice & Speech
The Juilliard School

paper•MEN: ISBN 0-936839-78-3
WOMEN: ISBN 0936839-79-1

THE REDUCED SHAKESPEARE COMPANY'S
COMPLEAT WORKS OF WLLM SHKSPR
(abridged)

by JESS BORGESON, ADAM LONG, and DANIEL SINGER

"ABSL HLRS." —*The Independent* (London)

"Shakespeare writ small, as you might like it! . . . Pithier-than-Python parodies . . . not to be confused with that august English company with the same initials. This iconoclastic American Troupe does more with less."

— *The New York Times*

"Shakespeare as written by *Reader's Digest*, acted by Monty Python, and performed at the speed of the Minute Waltz. So Forsooth! Get thee to the RSC's delightfully fractured *Compleat Works*."

— *Los Angeles Herald*

$8.95 • PAPER • ISBN 1-55783-157-2

SHAKESPEARE'S PLAYS IN PERFORMANCE by John Russell Brown

In this volume, John Russell Brown snatches Shakespeare from the clutches of dusty academics and thrusts him centerstage where he belongs—in performance.

Brown's thorough analysis of the theatrical experience of Shakespeare forcibly demonstrates how the text is brought to life: awakened, colored, emphasized, and extended by actors and audiences, designers and directors.

"A knowledge of what precisely can and should happen when a play is performed is, for me, the essential first step towards an understanding of Shakespeare."
—*from the Introduction by John Russell Brown*

paper•ISBN 1-55783-136-X•